Best Wishes!

THE
CHRIST
REPORT

THE
CHRIST
REPORT

A Novel

by

James Michael Pratt

New York Times Bestselling Author of The Last Valentine & The Lighthouse Keeper

Library of Congress Cataloging-in-Publication Data is available from the Library of Congress

Catalogue Data Pending

ISBN 0-9677764-1-4

HEARTLAND BOOKS

PowerThink Publishing
2020 Fieldstone Pkwy Ste. 900
Franklin, TN. 37069

Visit us at www.powerthink.com

Printed in the United States of America

10 9 8 7 6 5 4 3 2 1

Acknowledgments

The concept for *The Christ Report* was born in April 1998 while on a book tour for *The Last Valentine*. After several major publishing looks – Heartland Books of Franklin, Tennessee, a PowerThink Publishing LLC imprint, embraced it.

My appreciation to friends Carlos and Keri Packard, Mark and LaDawn Kastleman, Evan Fredrickson cover designer extraordinaire, Mandy Marie and Steve Eldredge, Steven Anderson editor, and all those early believers in this story of a man in search of redemption, love, and belief in the timeless story of the Holy Birth and Passion of the Christ.

TABLE OF CONTENTS

Prologue

A Secret Hidden

***

A secret kept since the Holy Birth will be revealed when two men, separated by two thousand years in time, search for a meaning greater than themselves. Both suffer from broken hearts, yearn to keep the women they love, and worry about their legacy. One, Sam Robertson, the world-famous host of CNTV's *The Sam Robertson Report*, will soon find that only a life-saving miracle can bring him the hope his sense of self-importance cannot offer.

The other man, battered by regrets as ancient as the biblical story in which he played a key role, once was an innkeeper – indeed, the very one who had rejected the parents of an infant destined to become immortalized as the Son of God in countless pageants and dramas. Now it's the innkeeper's charge to convey a vital message to the world, a message that has been kept hidden for two millennia.

This secret, kept even from those who understand the stories of the Holy Birth and the Passion, was not so much a secret that must not be known, but, rather, something *sacred*, kept hidden for so long because of mankind's self-serving stubbornness.

Now, not only will Sam land the interview of a lifetime, but he'll win another chance at life and love. And Cleopas the Innkeeper will likewise gain a second opportunity to redeem his soul and clear his name as the most vilified innkeeper of all time.

Their secret? It is only to be found in *The Christ Report*.

The Holy Birth

***

And all went to be taxed, everyone into his own city. And Joseph also went up from Galilee out of the city of Nazareth, into Judea, unto the city of David, which is called Bethlehem– to be taxed with Mary his espoused wife, being great with child.

And she brought forth her firstborn son, and wrapped him in swaddling cloths, and laid him in a manger; because there was no room for them in the inn.

Gospel of Luke Chapter 2 - King James New Testament

Easter Morning

***

And, behold, two of them went that same day to a village called Emmaus... and they talked together of all these things which had happened. And it came to pass, that, while they communed together and reasoned, Jesus himself drew near, and went with them. But their eyes were holden that they should not know him.

And he said unto them, What manner of communications are these that ye have one to another, as ye walk, and are sad?

And the one of them, whose name was Cleopas, answering said unto him, Art thou only a stranger in Jerusalem?

And they drew nigh unto the village, whither they went: and he made as though he would have gone further. But they constrained him, saying, Abide with us, for the day is far spent. And he went in to tarry with them.

Gospel of Luke Chapter 24 - King James New Testament

1

THE INNKEEPER

Bethlehem – Eve of Roman Emperor Augustus tax census

"More wine. And more loaves!" growled a legionnaire.

"See to it, Phinnias," the innkeeper whispered.

"Yes, Master Cleopas."

The usual mix at occasions of celebration and feasts in the land roundabout Jerusalem brought all sorts to this place. This night was no exception. The inn had filled to the brim with road-weary guests. Now the Emperor's edict, the Roman tax census, had brought thousands of additional visitors. The young innkeeper gazed across the raucous dining hall, filled beyond capacity. The required reporting of each head of house to his hometown or village of birth had made the inn of Cleopas at Bethlehem, not many furlongs from mighty Jerusalem itself, to nearly burst at the seams with all-night boarders.

"The fool thinks this is old wine. See how he pretends at drunkenness," Phinnias whispered into the ear of the server boy Asa, peering out over the sea of gruff legionnaires. The youth nodded and hurried past him with fresh loaves for each table.

People Cleopas had never seen before were swarming to Bethlehem to be counted. In fact, on the morrow, he himself would venture to Emmaus, the place of his own birth some three-score furlongs from the capital city in the opposite direction, where he would be tallied and made to pay the tax of a single man. Then, hurrying back once more, he would manage the crowds here.

He longed to stay in Emmaus – to, alas, be with her – but this throng promised to fill his purse. And revenue was much needed at the time. The guests packed into his dining hall and small inn eagerly relaxed their purse strings as they merrily consumed more wine, ate more victuals. Cleopas's job was to continue to stir up that merriment, to keep it going strong late into the evening. Soon he would have the dowry required by Jarom to ask for his daughter's hand in marriage. The sound of payment for his services in coins of copper, silver and gold, made the weariness of this night more bearable. He would rather be in Emmaus now, with her, but for this.

Yet another worry bore heavily on the innkeeper's youthful shoulders this night: Jarom, his future father-in-law, would be arriving at the inn any minute. Would he measure up to the man's expectations? He had already proven adept at turning a copper penny into a good shekel. Yet his lack of experience and firsthand knowledge of finance, of running such an elaborate establishment, was still very limited.

Barely twenty years old, recently inheriting this inn and boarding house from his uncle Simeon, Cleopas had never before been subject to such harsh demands. Like a father, Simeon had brought him up to learn a trade and be an observant Jew, quick to obey all the laws of the prophets. Although originally from the smaller Emmaus, Simeon had brought young Cleopas to Bethlehem after the death of the boy's parents.

From his eighth year the lad had worked at the inn, attended school, made his offerings, and observed the Sabbath. So close to Jerusalem, Cleopas - to Simeon's delight and regret alike - also had picked up on the varied cosmopolitan pretenses of travelers who stopped for refreshment on their way to the cities and coasts of other lands.

Cleopas, for instance, had mastered the diplomatic art of the smile, and of compromise. *The patron is always right*, Simeon often reminded him. *Satisfy thy guest, and thy purse shall never be empty*, was another favorite aphorism. And Cleopas had found in it much wisdom. And so it was that he carried on in Simeon's wise traditions.

Cleopas had proven shrewd for business, which pleased Simeon greatly. On several occasions before his death, the frail old man had put the duties of his entire hospitality enterprise atop the bony back of his young nephew. Cleopas, in turn, had never let him down. Simeon's wife had died of the fever years before, and, childless, Simeon's last wish was for Cleopas to inherit the inn. With his dying breath he had uttered: *"Remember, my son, there is always room at the inn for the least to the greatest. Walk with God. Peace be unto you, my son."*

So here he was, now; callow, on his own, yet having sworn to make this property even more prosperous, more famous for service than his well-respected Uncle Simeon had.

"More wine, I say! Innkeeper! The loaves! Where in the name of Jupiter, Zeus, and...and..." The unruly legionnaire turned to a fellow soldier, now pretending to be too drunk to know the difference between the question and the answer. "What is the Hebrews' name for their God?" The stammering soldier snickered to his company of friends, as if he'd just imparted the wittiest joke ever invented. Then, his comrades having shrugged off the babbled query, he bellowed his question to the roomful of guests.

No answer. The hall went silent as the diners pondered what injury the irrational man might do with his sword.

"No matter," he cackled loudly. "Bring the meats!" He slammed his fist down on the table and slumped back in his seat, sputtering a ribald string of harmless epithets in his native tongue.

"Soldiers," Cleopas muttered with disdain. But not just any soldiers. These were the most despised of the Roman Legion - Provincials. And they were late. Their custom was to set out for the Fortress Antonia at dusk. Perhaps they were camping in the fields this night, in anticipation of manning the census tables on the morrow. *Perhaps*, Cleopas grumbled.

You could never tell, though, about the occupiers. Uncertainty was one thing he, Cleopas, had come to count on. And these were of the crude Syrian band of legionnaires. Conscripts - no lovers of the Jew. Even if the Roman considered the Jew as a mere conquered people, conflict between the crass Syrians from the north and the Jews from the land of Israel went back many generations; blood, wars and strife had long cemented them as bitter enemies.

Now, however, both Syrian and Israelite alike were under Roman dominion. But each of the two nations regarded its captor from a differing viewpoint. On the one hand, the Jew only sought to free himself from cruelty and servitude; the Syrian, on the other hand, gladly picked up the sword for the Roman Legions, eagerly took his pay, a fine uniform, respect as a fellow conqueror - and occasionally made good on the opportunity to kill a Jew.

In a word, the Syrian joined in the ruthless game; the Jew picked up the sword for no conqueror.

This Syrian sort was the most vulgar guest Cleopas had known for many months; he was also the most prone to violence. Cleopas knew he must attend to this one, or the entire room of guests would know the Syrian's searing wrath.

"Now!" he barked again, pounding his fist even harder against the tabletop's long, wooden planks.

"Coming, sir! Yes, sir! Bringing a fresh loaf, a warm loaf, direct from the hearth," Cleopas called out. "The best loaf and the finest wine! Be assured, sir, I want only the best for you!"

The room grew deathly still: no rattling of a dish, nary a cough, no one dared breathe. All eyes were fastened upon the gruff, red-faced Syrian. The fate of every diner and boarder of this cozy hall rested upon the outcome of this bristling madman.

After several tense moments, the slovenly soldier hunched slightly forward, picked up a napkin, and dabbed at the corner of his mouth – now dripping with the last ounce of wine from his cup – and stuffed it with the last morsels of meat on his plate. He let out a drunken groan, as the soldier next to him spoke in the foreign tongue. Then they both chuckled. A snarl, a wave for the boy to hurry, and a look of contempt for this crowd was the answer from the troublemaker.

"Take this wine, take this bread, and satisfy the dogs," Cleopas whispered to Phinnias. "Do not be far from them. Be there when the Syrian pig grunts, mutters any word of aggravation. This busiest of nights, the gifts left upon the tables after the meal, our very reputation...all depend upon the satisfaction of these barbarians. We must ensure that their evening is warm and filling." Cleopas's eyes darted about the hall. He nodded at the mass of humanity filling the room, the average citizen maintaining cautious distance between himself and the body of soldiers. "Look at them. They are as eager as you and I to make sure these barbarians, these uncircumcised curs, are well attended to."

Phinnias nodded. Cleopas shook his head, trying to jolt away the sleepiness weighing him down. He could hardly keep his eyes from drooping shut. Even his smile was losing its edge; his act, his well-practiced, happy-host, glad-to-be-a-servant-to-all manner was flagging badly. He had but three hours' sleep the night before, arising early to go to market and start the cooking fires in the hearths pegged alongside the sleeping quarters.

Cleopas gazed up at the rows of Hebrew words carved in a horizontal piece of wood hung above the inn's door. There on the white fir plank brought from a forest in Lebanon, was written the summation of a significant story.

It had taken place years ago. A gracious, youthful family - kin to Simeon, father and son, former Bethlehem residents but now carpenters from upper Galilee - they had not only repaired tables and chairs to pay for their room and board during Passover, but had carved the wooden plaque as a gesture of gratitude. Simeon had cherished the simple gift ever since, declaring that it should hang there forever so that whenever a boarder came or went through the door, he or she would be compelled to read it.

Cleopas had been a table boy, a server, one week into his eighth year from the time he had first been brought to the inn. Cousins of Simeon, the man and his son had made the pilgrimage at the Passover in the year the boy - Joseph, by name - had become a man. Cleopas recalled watching as Joseph carefully chiseled the words into the soft rectangular piece of wood. Joseph was the son of Jacob, also a carpenter. This Joseph now would be four years older than Cleopas. Simeon cherished these words from the *Koheleth* - words from he who was simply called "the Preacher." The innkeeper strained to read them. Tired eyes studied the message reminding him of his duty.

Go thy way, eat and drink with joy, and drink thy wine with a merry heart, for God now accepteth thy works. Live joyfully with the wife whom thou lovest, for that is thy portion in this life.

Cleopas wasn't sure if God accepted his works or not, but he was sure that his inn, situated on the road leading into and through Bethlehem, would be the inn of choice for many a weary traveler. This establishment would likewise provide for his future bride, Mary, daughter of Jarom of Emmaus, a fellow innkeeper and a first cousin to Uncle Simeon.

Cleopas had long loved the slender, comely young lady. Flaxen, her crown was made of soft, silken braids with tresses so fine, falling loosely upon delicate shoulders, as if to accentuate the sculpted beauty of the face one would expect of a princess. Wispy locks with a hint of crimson, they seemed willing to fly free in the stirrings of a soft spring breeze, in perfect harmony with the cheerful songs that so effortlessly fell from her lips. Every mannerism, every thread of her earthy beauty beckoned him, called to him to touch... Still, Cleopas could not. Not as yet.

He yearned for the girl, now a woman of legal marrying age. He pictured her eyes, those extraordinarily remarkable eyes, a tint of olive, dark yet penetrating, gazing out from a face rivaling the purity of an angel. Fair skin, soft skin, in need of tender care, he longed to hold her hand in his, sit and marvel at the woman who would bare him sons and daughters.

A living gem, Mary was granted these rare refinements and qualities by the very God of Israel; He seemed to have touched her from the heavenly throne, making her every feature and attribute stand out for him, Cleopas, to see and love. Mary...the sound of the name thrilled him. Mary was the morning sun, bright, full of shimmer and shine, a sparkle to please those who came near. "Dear Mary," he breathed, unaware of his daydreaming solitude. "I must have her," he mouthed to himself, voicelessly adding, "and soon."

But first he must prove himself to Jarom, a rather stubborn man who no doubt would demand proof that the youthful innkeeper was capable of the task Simeon had left to him.

"The door! Answer the door, Asa!" commanded Cleopas, awakened from his reverie by the urgent pounding. "If it be Jarom, usher him quietly and without hesitation to the quarters reserved for him. But," he quickly warned the youth, "there is no room - no room in the inn for anyone else! Tell them there are victuals, but they must eat outside. No room! Make it clear, Asa!"

Cleopas hastened to the kitchen to see if the porridge was ready for the kettle, the mutton for the skewer. Any night but this one he would gladly accept another boarder.

Unbeknownst to anyone but he, Cleopas had, in fact, reserved one single room for some special guest that might happen by. It was his newest and best suite, fit for the High Priest, or a Roman Tribune. With all new furnishings, it was fitted with an ample basin for bathing, alongside urns of fresh water from the deep well for drinking. A commodious bed, fit for a king, with posts of cedar and side rails as well, graced one wall. Lambs' wool – not straw, but thick pads of fleece – made up the forgiving bedding, allowing a traveler's tired body to find its most satisfying slumber.

The room was spacious, nearly one-half the size of the dining hall. And two separate chambers resided on either side of the main room. His dear Mary and their children would one day occupy these fine dwellings.

And something else the largest of these rooms possessed, which no ordinary home in Bethlehem could boast: a window with glass! The only room to let in the light of the mighty city, God's City, bathed in the brilliance of the nearby temple and its golden fiery dome. The glory of God resting there, in such plain sight, would always remind them of their eternal love. Squinting through the fiery, molded silica, one could behold nearly the entire panorama. The window had been a gift from an artisan whose glass-blowing craft was prized throughout finer homes in Jerusalem. The man was from the Far East and occasionally traveled with the caravans of his friend Artemaus, who, when passing this way, often camped his people in the hilly fields skirting Bethlehem. But during his sojourn in the land roundabout Jerusalem, most often he came to reside at Cleopas's inn.

Cleopas had just that very week finished furnishing these rooms. *Chambers for a Prince*, he mused. Jarom would be pleased and would be the first to occupy this room. He would understand how special his daughter, Mary, was to him. And the master chamber would be her room one day – his Mary's room. He would serve her every want, her every whim. This night would prove to Jarom, her father, that he, Cleopas, would indeed make his daughter a suitable husband.

Cleopas paced back and forth, nearly working a path into the wooden floor. So much was riding on the events of the next few hours. A half-day's ride upon donkey, a full-day's walk from Emmaus, Jarom would arrive exhausted, for he would have suffered the same vagaries of this Roman edict: the Jews of Israel were to return to their place of birth to be numbered. So Jarom – surely to be followed the next morning by his family – for they too, had been ordered to appear for the census, should be here at any moment.

"Master Cleopas," Asa said, handing him a message. "From Jarom."

Cleopas excitedly unfolded the small parchment and read the few scrawled words. Then he read them again, a pall of disappointment creasing his face. "He's not coming. The morrow will see him by last hour, before twilight. He will come with his family to do his reporting for the census, then return straightway. He cannot stay," Cleopas sighed.

"Master, what does it mean?" Asa ventured, knowing full well the anxiety Cleopas had suffered this night. Asa was but five years younger than his master, an apprentice lad without family, and so what might affect this business and the life of Cleopas had a direct effect upon him as well.

"No need for worry, Asa. See the man there, the smartly dressed one? Notice his robes and the delicate, refined lady he accompanies?"

"Yes, Master."

"Make inquiries of him. He dresses after the manner of the publicans...a lawyer, perhaps. Inquire whether he is staying in Bethlehem for the tax reporting, and if he should need a room. I may as well profit from this. Hurry, go!" Cleopas could make quite a sum for the single, elegantly adorned room he had reserved for Jarom – as much as he made on all ten of the sleeping rooms together. He nervously looked on as Asa described the amenities. The ornately clothed man smiled, then arose, speaking softly to his female companion.

Husband and wife, Cleopas reasoned. *Reporting for the census, no doubt... From Caesarea; used to the finest. They probably share some cramped, drab room with mother and father here in town. We'll see,* he thought as he watched Asa part the curtain leading to the suite. *Good. They will not be able to resist.*

A few tense moments lapsed. *Asa should be back by now,* the innkeeper said to himself. He resumed his pacing, eyeing, as was his habit, the servers filling the needs of his other guests, listening to the rhythmic clanging of pots, dishes, goblets, amid the din of conversation and bawdy prattle of the Syrians. Across the hall he spotted Phinnias, attending to their whims; the mass of merchants and regular diners feasting at the tables...all gave off the sounds of money being made – and Cleopas was addicted to that sound.

A knock came upon the door.

"Phinnias!" Cleopas called out to the table waiter, urgently pointing to the door.

8

Phinnias shrugged, his hands filled with an assortment of platters and plates. To make matters worse, the same Syrian soldier was once again hammering the table with his fists, berating the exasperated waiter while his companions laughed and jeered. Cleopas only could wag his head, signaling that he understood Phinnias's dilemma. He had to tend to the rantings of the barbarian.

"Oh, stop. Yes, yes, I'm coming!" he shouted. He could barely hear himself over the cries of the boisterous crowd. The noise, the laughter, the raucous behavior of both soldier and citizen, all of it only seemed amplified the more wine that was poured.

Cleopas unlatched the thick, wooden door and swung it open. The man outside, dressed in rough, homespun tunic, appealed to him with an expression of panic and hurried speech. Cleopas sensed the fear, the desperation in this man's eyes, and knew what he would have to say. Still, he let him go on.

"Sir, I beseech you. This is our third stop of the evening. My wife is with child. Is Simeon in? Can I speak to him?"

"You know Simeon?"

"I have not seen him for many years. But I once stayed here with my father, the year I reported to the temple, the year I became a man."

"I am Cleopas. Simeon is with God - just one year ago now. Simeon was my uncle. I came to dwell with him in my eighth year."

"Then you are kin," the tired man sighed, relaxing a bit. "You are the serving lad I remember," he added. "But such a fine man now. I am Joseph ben Jacob, here to report for the census. This is my wife..."

Cleopas forced a smile, then held up his hand, a gesture meant to halt the man's feeble pleadings. The innkeeper realized his only available room was a costly one, being admired even at this very moment by one who would pay a small fortune, a king's ransom, to take proper care of the lovely lady at the table.

Joseph, his weight nervously shifting from one foot to the other, resumed his entreaty. "Can you spare a room for one night? We can pay. I am from Galilee and she cannot ride another furlong. We must find a room, a midwife... Kind sir...dare I say kin? I don't know what to do."

"I - " Cleopas stumbled.

Joseph struggled in search of his purse. "I have..."

Cleopas once more raised his hand to calm the man, then turned to see Asa, nodding. *Good. Now I can honestly tell this man there is no room here.* Cleopas restated his refusal with mild tones, apologetic words.

The man, however, would have none of it. "But she is giving birth. Please, sir. You are kin of Simeon. We have no other family here. I must find shelter without delay. Simeon surely would not have..."

"Friend! I will not stand here and have you invoke the sentiments I have for my deceased uncle, sentiments close to my heart," replied Cleopas, pounding a closed fist upon his chest for emphasis. "As I said, there is no room at this inn this night. Look for yourself." He stepped back and held the door open wide.

Cleopas nodded toward the finely dressed lawyer and his lady. The lawyer held out his hand and his wife reached up. He whispered something that pleased her greatly, and then with Asa leading the way, entered beyond the curtain separating the dining hall from the sleeping quarters. The hall itself was lined with tables, surrounded by loud diners and hired servers frantically trying to keep goblets filled, delivering bowls hot with soups, stews of mutton.

"Sir..." the voice of the man choked. "Mary cannot ride another minute. See her pain." He motioned toward the woman. "Give us a place outside the kitchen, anywhere...please..."

Cleopas, for the first time, glanced over at the pain-faced figure atop the donkey. "Mary?" he asked. *I have a Mary,* he thought. She was to be here in the morning. "Mary, you say?"

"Yes. Mary, my wife. She is young. I must attend to her needs with dignity..."

Cleopas's compassion at last began to conquer his reason. Perhaps he could let them have *his* room. *No, I must be here for the lawyer, now; nearby to attend to his needs, coax more for the service I will provide. I cannot...*

He himself had slept in the stable on more than one occasion. The straw was clean. He was a man who would rent his own room for that extra shekel, that single, blessed coin that would bring him closer to his aim of providing Jarom with a proper dowry to win the hand of his daughter. *Mary,* he thought.

10

"Sir, look above your door," Joseph pointed. "I hung it there myself," he added to encourage Cleopas's growing sense of sympathy.

The desperate man's words shook Cleopas from his mental wanderings. He stood back and read the hand-carved sign that Simeon had insisted remain in place forever.

"It is rented," Asa whispered in Cleopas's ear. "And for twice the asking price," he added, a trace of pride in his voice. "Master, there is no room," Asa reminded him, noting his master's silent, stupor-like reverie, considering the desperate couple, the door ajar...

"Shut the door, Innkeeper!" growled the Syrian. "Are you a fool? I said – "

But Cleopas wasn't listening. He was in that oblivious mind-space where people go sometimes, the narrow corridor of consciousness, a place where memories remind one of similar times and their outcomes. *What would Simeon do? Give up his room?* He considered what that meant. *How many days?* Simeon was kin. *That makes me kin,* he reminded himself.

I am a businessman, not a charity, he counseled his conscious. He pictured the woman he loved, then his gaze once more swung back to the weeping woman seated upon the donkey. "Asa," he mumbled under his breath, "take care of this place. I am going to the stable. Send one of the servers for the midwife Anna. Have her come to the stable immediately. Have the server then bring cloth – and bedding, any extra bedding from storage."

"But Cleopas, Master, I – "

"Asa! Do as I say, now!"

The boy nodded and retreated.

"Come," Cleopas urged, and reached for the arm of the man. "I have shelter to give you without cost. There is clean straw and I am ordering adequate bedding for you."

The Galilean replied gratefully, blessing the name of Simeon, Cleopas and all his household as he led the animal with his quietly sobbing wife away from the boarding house.

Joseph ben Jacob of Nazereth. Well...

He knew Simeon would have wanted him to keep peace at the inn. And, under ordinary circumstances - not these pressures of the Roman census - he would have found some accommodation, even if it were his own living quarters.

But this is no ordinary night, he whispered to himself.

2

SAM ROBERTSON REPORTS

"Cardinal," he began. "What would you consider the most important event in all of world history?" Sam Robertson asked.

"Two days must vie equally as the greatest. Christmas, the day the Son of God took a mortal body, and of course the day he reclaimed it, that day of the immortal resurrection known as Easter morn," answered Cardinal McIntyre, a special Vatican guest to the nightly talk show.

Robertson nodded. "Let us, then, agree that the man Jesus of Nazareth was born of Mary at Bethlehem. And let us also agree that he has been and is worshipped by many as the Son of God. Historically, the evidence and witnesses weigh heavily in favor of the biblical account of his birth, his life, and what his admirers thought of him. And excuse me if I play the devil's advocate here, Cardinal, but why do you feel that Easter should be considered one of the two greatest historical events? After all, there is no hard proof that a literal resurrection actually took place, just hearsay witnesses some two thousand years dead...if they even existed then," Sam hinted with smug cynicism.

Robertson's religious guest avoided the bait thrown his way, responding, "Two witnesses in any court of law make a compelling case. We have dozens of witnesses who saw him after he arose from the dead." The Cardinal smiled politely, letting his words sink in a bit. "That being the case, the hope of immortality which Easter morn represents makes it, in my view, the single most important day and event in world history, along with the Lord's birth."

"Well, until I interview God himself, I'm afraid I'm not swayed." Sam had found himself blurting out the words before he could weigh the impact such a statement might have on his guest and the viewing public. "After all," he plowed ahead, "wouldn't it be more practical to consider the harnessing of electricity, providing light to the world, or something tangible, something that's done so much good, as one of the world's greatest events or achievements? I mean, look at that. In a mere one hundred years of the incandescent light bulb, we have achieved more advances in all areas of technology than the previous six thousand years combined! With all due respect, of course."

"Of course," Cardinal McIntyre nodded, his face tightening into a near-scowl. "And more killing, destruction, and sorrow. Harnessing energy, providing light to the world, is a poor substitute for he who *is* the *Light of the World,* Sam." Then he extended his hand across the interview table and said, "It's been a privilege to be with you this evening."

Somewhat stunned that the Cardinal had abruptly terminated the interview several minutes short, Sam accepted the proffered hand, smiled, and turned to camera 2. "This concludes our weeklong visit with guests representing major religious denominations, this, the final week of November." Then he turned one last time to his guest and added, "Cardinal McIntyre, it has been an honor having you with us. May you have a very special Christmas – and please give my regards to his Excellency, the Pope." That said, he turned to face camera 1. "I will be taking Thanksgiving week off to celebrate a very special event with my wife. I hope you'll join our guest hosts, some of Hollywood's elite, including my good friends Clint Eastwood, Tom Hanks, Harrison Ford, and singer Faith Hill, and Naomi Judd. May your family enjoy the coming national day of gratitude, Thanksgiving Day, with safety and love. From all of us here at *The Sam Robertson Report,* good evening, and God bless."

The red light blinked off and both figures sagged back into their seats. "You say 'God bless' like you mean it," Cardinal McIntyre remarked, now they were off the air. "You do fear God, don't you, Samuel?"

Robertson was taken aback. No one called him *Samuel* anymore. "A figure of speech. Of course, if there is a God," he shrugged. "I do mean it...and I fear him.... I guess," he added with a laugh.

"Fear can be healthy," the Cardinal interjected. "It can provide motivation to find him."

"Fears are not convenient, your Grace. They make you think of unpleasant things, things that belong to the dead and the damned."

"Samuel," the Cardinal sighed, not unkindly. "You are forgetting his other words: *Peace I give you, my peace I leave with you. Let not your heart be troubled neither let it be afraid.*"

Robertson wrinkled the bridge of his nose as if to ward off some awful stench. "I've got everything I ever wanted. No troubled heart here," he said, thumping his chest with the tip of his finger.

"You do not understand the wholeness that true peace offers. I will pray for you." The tinge of a smile crossed the Cardinal's lips.

"That is an offer I will not refuse, your Grace. By the way...I was a bit shocked that you signed us off like that, cutting the interview short. I'm used to being in control. But I admire that," he said, grinning in return. "May I ask why you ended our interview early?"

"I never debate reality," he answered.

"I've offended you?"

"No. But I will not be put on the defensive. You must learn who is really in control. I just thought I'd offer a small lesson," the Cardinal said, his smile widening.

"You feel it was sacrilegious of me to state my skepticism?"

"No, everyone is entitled to their beliefs. Rest assured, my good friend, that God knows you, and one day there shall be an interview with him. When that will be and who will interview who is the question."

"I respect that, sir, and, believe me, I would love nothing more than to be sure of what you call *reality*. Seeing is believing, as they say."

"No, Samuel. Faith is not stirred from seeing, but from here." The Cardinal lightly patted the space over his heart. "Sam," he started again, "why don't you join us for a special Nativity celebration in Rome. I would be happy to make the arrangements. This year's sacred festivity promises to be exceptional."

"Thank you for the offer, Cardinal McIntyre. I'm honored. But I have an *exceptional* Christmas celebration of my own planned. I've been married one year now and we'll be spending our first Christmas together in seclusion — and being a little stingy, I guess. Rachel's college-age son will be at the grandparents' place. So it'll be just the two of us — definitely a *no-room-at-the-inn* style celebration."

"Well, in that case, may I offer you my blessing for a long and happy life together," the Catholic Father offered in parting.

"Thank you. I need all the help I can get."

***

Down deep, Sam Robertson, the Jersey-born-and-bred host of the CNTV nightly interview show, knew there wasn't much left in him. He'd suffered three minor and one major heart attack over the past fifteen years, and had undergone double bypass surgery ten years ago.

His had been a hard life, and he supposed there was no one to blame but himself for the condition his old ticker was in. For years he'd resorted to alcohol, partying, and any type of cover-up to mask the broken heart... Sam could hardly complete the thought, one that had ricocheted around in his head all these years. For so long he'd struggled to find the *right* one, the woman who would complete him, make him whole – to no avail. He imagined that his broken spirit had given him ample justification to be hard on his body over the years.

As far as the broadcast world went, well, there wasn't much left for him to do, unless, as he jokingly told a former colleague from CNBC – and now Cardinal McIntyre, as well – unless he was to land an interview with God himself.

A wearisome, fast-paced four decades of television journalism, beginning with the Kennedy assassination coverage in '63, had taken a terrible toll on his health – not to mention on his relationships.

Now, with a worldwide adoring audience, Sam couldn't really be sure who truly cared about him, or why. *Was it his fame, notoriety, money?* He had asked himself that question a thousand times, particularly each time he met an attractive woman who showed any sign of interest in him.

Three failed marriages and six grown children later, Sam had finally met the girl of his dreams, Rachel Adams, though he wondered if she could ever love a man with so many miles on him. Why should she care for *him*? Money? *Could be...*

Or maybe it was his charm. But with all the young, hunky, wavy-haired smooth-talkers in the business, why should she choose him? Thousands of interviews had left his face with a world-weary, drawn, careworn look, far from the chiseled features he once had. *Yeah, it had to be the money.*

Nine million dollars per year in salary and nearly a dozen commercial endorsements – from milk to therapeutic mattresses – had set him up for life. No way could he spend it fast enough, even after his ex-wives got theirs.

Rachel was everything all the other women had been, and more. She possessed something discernibly different, a class and character that made her stand above the others. She lit up a room. He noticed it from the first time they met at a dinner reception in downtown Manhattan's Ritz-Carlton. The reception had been in honor of Terry Warner, a CNTV reporter who, after two years of being held hostage in Mogadishu, had been freed during a firefight between warring Somali clans and turned over to a negotiator from the U.N.

Rachel was indeed different. Right from the start she'd treated him with courtesy and respect. In fact, Sam mused, that was the way she treated everyone she met. Perhaps that was it. She exuded such genuine warmth. A senior editor with *U.S. News Weekly*, she was simply dignified, and obviously well thought of by everyone in the business.

"She's untouchable, Sam," Kit Bronson had noted under his breath as he brushed past him at the reception. He guessed Kit had noticed him eyeing her.

"We'll see about that," he'd shot back over his shoulder, setting his drink down and sauntering over to the gaggle of four laughing, joking younger men who'd flocked around her.

"Miss Adams?" he began, ignoring the others vying for her attentions. "I was wondering if you might like to spend a few minutes out in the fresh air. I'm taking a stroll in Central Park and would be pleased at your company."

"Why certainly, Mr. Robertson," she'd beamed. "Please allow me to excuse myself."

The four GQ-cover-boy-model cub reporters appeared stunned at the old man's bravado...and apparent victory.

"Don't look so down, boys," he chuckled under his breath so only they could hear him. "It takes time to know what a woman's really looking for." Then he winked across the room to Kit and escorted Rachel from the party, wrap in hand.

It had been a glorious spring evening, the normally grimy New York City air freshly cleansed by a light mist. The Ritz-Carlton, located on 59th and across the street from Central Park, made it easy for Sam to flag down one of the ever-present horse-drawn carriages. She gripped his hand as he helped her up into the seat. "I imagine it's hard to maintain any sort of anonymity around here."

Sam, struggling to keep his composure, merely stammered, "Yes, it is." He couldn't help but be distracted – mesmerized, actually – by Rachel's style and elegance. "Although New Yorkers aren't easily impressed," he added in an effort to restore some measure of poise.

After an awkward silence, Rachel spoke up. "Well, this is nice," she said, smiling. Her eyes flitted about the park grounds. "Reminds me of why I like New York so much."

"Oh, why is that?" Sam probed.

"There's always a surprise around every corner." Her answer had been the sort expected from a cheerful, Pollyanna-like girl. He was entranced by the naive curiosity and wonder she radiated.

"Indeed," he replied, chuckling to himself. He felt like a schoolboy, so much putty in her hands, if she wanted it that way.

They jostled along quietly for some time, finally breaking the stillness with niceties about their respective homes, families, and what had brought her to her new assignment at *U.S. News Weekly*.

"From Colorado. Grew up in Memphis through the '70s, though," she'd said. While her father had worked for the Interior Department, she'd traveled with him, acquiring an interest in affairs relating to the western states. Now she covered the western United States on environment and state governmental issues, settling in to Denver right out of college.

Sam's memory-bank of newscasts long-past clicked into gear. "I was a guest once of Elvis; right before he died. Later in the '80's I did a music 'special' on 'the King.' Would you believe it? Graceland... King... Almost sounds religious. Seems so long ago now. Then I hosted the Memphis Youth Symphony Christmas program back in 19...gosh, it's been awhile."

"1985," she broke in. "It was Christmas week of '85. I was there."

"You were?" The words tumbled out in a boyish rush.

"I was a member of the Youth Symphony Orchestra," she explained.

"Uh oh," he mumbled. He shook his head and laughed.

"What's wrong?"

"Me. It's just me," he breathed.

"Did I say something wrong?"

"No. Certainly not." He turned back towards her. "May I ask what you thought of me then. I guess you were in your teens?"

"I was a High School Senior. I told my mother I hoped I'd marry a man like you someday," she blurted out – then immediately looked away, embarrassed by her sudden revelation.

Stunned, the smile on his face turned to absolute shock. "I was much older, even then," he muttered, as much to himself as to her.

"Probably three or four times older...but only half as old now," she offered, seeking to recover from the gaff.

Sam quickly rescued her as he did the math aloud. They both laughed.

Sam couldn't believe where he was and what he was doing right then. This woman – this young, young woman – was amazing. She seemed possessed of a true, unadulterated guileless nature. So rare, the pure quality of goodness appeared to be her most noticeable characteristic. He was eager to know why. He asked if she would see him the next day.

"I'm sorry. Sunday is kind of special to me," replied Rachel. "I promised my son Michael we'd attend church and hang out together. He's out of school on spring break, and I've found it necessary to balance out all the other influences of the week by being strict in that area. You know, keeping one day to myself. But, perhaps another time. Here's my number..."

***

The courtship had been glorious. Highly unusual, so Sam thought, but splendidly glorious. She wouldn't let him touch her outside of kisses and snuggling together in front of the evening fire at her place. He'd met the family in Colorado, and had been accepted as warmly as he could have ever dreamed. There was some trauma over the age difference, but, once everyone had settled down, he was treated like family.

It was the minor heart attack that next spring that had been the shocker, a wake-up call leaving him flat on his back, helpless, in the coronary care unit and wondering if Rachel would want a used-up, spent old man who might never even be able to jog around the block with her.

"We're going to change your diet," she'd declared matter-of-factly when she came to visit.

"You'll still marry me?" he uttered in disbelief.

"Of course!" she'd exclaimed, leaning down and kissing him on the forehead. "Get some rest. I'll see you tomorrow."

This girl had faith in him, but also a higher level of belief in something else, something beyond this world of fear, tumult, and even...death.

But it was the "final curtain" of life's drama that Sam Robertson was most afraid of. The calendar turning a young *60-something* on him this year, and being married to a 40 year-old beauty queen, meant the concept of death held something for him it hadn't before. It would take her away from him when it happened. *"If I die..."* he'd mumbled to himself hundreds of times now, always unable to finish the sentence.

Time, he pondered, was against him by reason of his insurance company's mortality tables, if nothing else. And mortality tables didn't lie. Dozens of friends on the other side of the great unknown proved them accurate.

Sam would be happy to believe that something out there existed, especially if it meant he could have a few more years than the doctors were telling him he had. Bad heart, prostate cancer, failing lungs... *What kind of God ruled this planet of death, disease and broken hearts?*

He often asked his guests this question, sometimes couching it as follow-up to an especially profound answer. His interviewees were all the great ones of the world: presidents, senators, generals, sports stars, actors and actresses, musicians, magicians, kings, queens, princes, tyrants and spiritual leaders.

Major and minor religious icons the likes of Billy Graham, James Dobson, Pat Robertson, the Dalai Lama, high-ranking Baptist ministers, Mormon authorities...even the Pope in Rome had once granted him an interview and been a guest on his program. And all had a common thread running through their answers to his keynote question: *"Do you believe there is a God and, if so, why does he allow so much misery?"*

"Yes, Sam, I believe there is a God and that he allows individual freedom to action. It is man who fails the test, not God," seemed to be the collective, composite reply, as if each had been a collaborator in the answer.

Too simplistic for Sam. Too easy; a universal cop-out, basically. So with Rachel in his life, and he wrapped up in her unreasonable love for him – with all the age difference, his chronic though kept-under-wraps battle with poor health, his complete comfort with having acknowledged the possibility of a supreme force yet dismissing any actual belief in a God – what would he ever be able to do to satisfy her? How could he ever measure up to her lofty expectations?

And, most importantly, how could he ever be assured of even one more glorious year by her side? He cared for her with all the youthful stirrings of a love-struck kid, despite what his aging body betrayed. To have five, ten more years assured; for that he'd sell his soul.

He'd given up smoking the year before and, except for a glass of wine with his evening meals, all other vices had been surrendered. He wanted to live forever now, enjoy every moment he could with Rachel. Now he could only be concerned about one day – today – and live it marvelously happy while he could with his beautiful and very-much-alive wife.

3

DEAD MEN DON'T LIE

More and more lately, his daily thoughts all seemed to bend back towards his own unbelief. The more he tried to challenge the faith of another, the more he realized that his own faith remained on shaky ground. Though a self-proclaimed agnostic, his own immortality was now a front-and-center concern, in spite of logic. Logic said that when you're dead, you're dead. He'd never known of anyone who, having died, had come back to talk about it. He certainly would have been delighted to interview such a person if given the chance. He'd sat with mediums, folks who claimed communication with souls beyond the grave, but that wasn't the real deal. He'd prefer a ghost, someone to talk to who *had* lived once, to give him the straight scoop on things.

Dead men don't lie. But they don't come back to tell the truth, either, he reasoned. And he had interviewed many a person who now was nothing more than a celluloid memory. Their images were archived in his vaults, where his *Sam Robertson Reports* were stored on videotape, catalogued by date.

Sam had given notice just the week before. His producers were not at all happy by the suddenness of it all, but it was in the contract in plain black and white: *A two-month notice for any reason of ill health and only one week of remaining interviews if his doctors would approve of studio work.*

The competition was heavy: his good pal and friendly rival Larry King, the perennial and ageless Geraldo Rivera, Lou Dobbs, the sometimes acerbic but entertaining Bill O'Reilly, and the smooth younger commentators of radio and cable like Sean Hannity and Glenn Beck. All turned up the heat.

Network competition for viewers was a never-ending battle. No matter how long he worked, how hard, Sam Robertson was still needed to boost ratings. His CNTV producer Mary Kelly had made it her personal mission to keep him from walking. "Just one more year," she'd say. But now even she, his most staunch advocate, had given up hope. Now she seemed flattened, stunned by the news.

"I'm sick and I'm tired, Mary. I need to quit at the top, not six feet under," he'd told her. She wasn't being realistic, he'd argued. He had delivered his medical file to the CNTV execs, and she knew of his bouts with heart disease and the prostate cancer – his latest surgery had made national headlines the year before. She really shouldn't have be so surprised. *What was Mary thinking, that he would live forever?* He winced at the thought.

Rachel was an angel. She'd gone ahead and married him even amid all these questions about his health. He went home every night like a puppy dog, wagging his tail, wondering how to please her, anxious to make her happy. And she seemed to be just that: happy. Yes, she really did seem content. He was trying not to deceive himself about it. After all, he was one of the best judges of character he knew. Certainly he had the right to be, having conducted a few thousand interviews. He woke up every morning out of his mind in love, trying to figure out how she could continue to be so in love with him. One of his former marriages hadn't even lasted this long.

But now, Sam realized he didn't even know what lay beyond the next week. He was scheduled for another battery of tests this coming Friday. What news would Doc Peterson deliver this time? That he had the heart of an 80-year-old and the lungs of a dead man? Peterson was always blunt, to the point, candid to a fault. He'd always appreciated it in the past, but now Sam would prefer a few good lies.

4

THE TEST

Sam entered the dressing room and traded in his suit, trademark sports shirt and bowtie for a set of blue pajama-like cotton trousers and matching short-sleeve shirt. He sighed heavily, wishing he were anywhere but here.

"How do I look, Maria?" He smiled a wincing smile as he sucked in his recently trimmed-at-the-waistline gut and placed his hands on hips in a Superman pose.

"Well, you still have Dudley Do-Right's chin!" the matronly nurse cackled as she led her pitiful patient down the antiseptically clean hallway.

Sam trailed behind her, deep in thought, his superhuman bravado deflated by reality's slap to the side of the head, and wanting desperately to have twenty-five years back.

Maria tried to brighten the moment. "Don't look so glum. Everything will be okay, Mister Robertson. You've trimmed down since the last time I saw you," she added with a wink.

"I lost weight, too," he mocked in response.

"We'll see about that. Step up to the scale." She toyed with the counterweights on the bar as the scale balanced. "169.5 pounds. My, my, you have lost a few more pounds."

"Told ya."

"Why the sudden urge to do what Doctor Petersen has been preaching for the last twenty years?"

He let out a deep, formerly nicotine-filled-lung-style cough. Then he shrugged. "Although we were face to face, the bathroom mirror and I weren't seeing eye to eye. I decided to make the first move."

She chuckled, smiled, and pointed to the chair.

"Ah, Maria, not the chair," he moaned.

She tore a long syringe out of its package and laid it on a tray nearby. "Which arm today, Mister Robertson?"

"Left," he sighed.

She tied the rubber band around his upper arm, restricting the flow of blood to reveal a blue-colored vein. "Here we go," she smiled. "Just a pinch. Try to be brave, Mr. Robertson," she giggled.

"You're getting a kick out of this aren't you?" he grumbled.

"Maria the Vampire, they called me in nursing school. You should know me by now. I never hurt you yet." She squinted and smiled as she worked to ease the needle into the vein. "Sorry, Mister Robertson. We'll have to try again. That was a good vein years ago when I first did this."

"I'll have your job," he whimpered.

"There we go. Just a little more..." She drew the needle from his arm and planted a cotton swab on the tender spot. "You keep being good like this and I'll get you a lollipop. Hold it tight until I come back." She picked up the blood sample and headed toward the lab down the hall, leaving him there to consider the day of tests ahead.

Rachel was supposed to meet him for dinner at Mario's on Park Avenue. He was looking forward to some indulgence after a whole year of abiding by a strict diet of vegetables, fish and other lean meats, skim milk, and no real alcohol. After dinner they'd spend the night at the place where they met, the Ritz-Carlton, followed by an uninterrupted week at a $2,000-per-day hide-a-way in the Bahamas.

Sam looked forward to focusing all his attentions on Rachel, on their future together and the love they shared. To be loved by her was more than the icing on the cake of a lifetime full of professional satisfaction. She was the cake, the reason he'd worked so hard for so long. *But why had it taken so long to find the love of his life?* His mind swirled around the question as he waited for Maria to take him through the remaining tests.

"This way, please, Mister Robertson," she motioned, awakening him from his musings.

"Treadmill?"

"Uh huh," she mumbled, smiling. "Here we go. Your own private exercise room– Rudy," she called to the technician in the room next door. "Let's hook Mister Robertson up. I'll shave," she giggled.

"You enjoy this job too much, Maria," Sam whined.

"Okay. Off with your shirt," she cooed, holding a double-edge razor in her hand.

"I'm going on my first anniversary honeymoon tonight. Please go light on the chest hair."

"I'm afraid you'll have to live with some bald spots," she answered merrily as she drew the razor's edge just inches over his left nipple. "Oops," she sounded startled. "Just kidding."

"Look, Maria. This is serious stuff. Go easy," he grumbled. "I'm serious!"

She stood back and gazed approvingly at her handiwork, like an artist would her canvas. "I don't think you look at all bad," she assured him.

"Ahh...what's the use. I didn't feel like taking my shirt off in public anymore anyway," he sarcastically groused.

"Ready to be wired, Mister Robertson?" Rudy asked as he wheeled the EKG machine up next to the treadmill.

Sam nodded.

"Okay. We'll start you out on an easy pace, then – "

"Yeah, yeah. I know the routine," Sam gestured. "Let's do it."

Rudy taped on the final probe, switched on the machine and began to monitor Sam's heart rate, blood pressure levels and all the rest.

Sam feigned disinterest, but did keep an eye on Rudy's face for any signs of concern with the readings he monitored on the real-time screen. The technician, however, stoically performed his duties. "Cranking up the treadmill. Any problems?"

Sam offered a "thumbs up" as his pace quickened to the demands of the wide, whirring band that caused his stride to lengthen.

"Okay, Mister Robertson. Going to speed it up just a bit more... How's the breathing? Dizzy, faint?"

"I'm fine, Rudy," Sam huffed.

A minute passed. "How am I doing, Rudy?" he asked as he got into the jogging portion of the treadmill test.

Rudy gave a slight nod as he studied the paper report issuing from the machine. "I think that's enough. I'm going to shut the machine down to a walk."

Sam stepped off the machine and bent over, hands on knees, to regain his breath. "That wasn't so bad," he panted.

Rudy patted his arm. "You just have a seat right here. Would you like to lie down?"

"No, I want to keep going – get these accursed exams over with. I've got a hot date..."

"You wait right here, I'll be back in a sec," said the technician, hurrying out of the room.

Sam didn't want to feel nervous over Rudy's abruptness, so he leaned back, head against the wall, and visualized himself and Rachel lying side by side on the shores of a mountain lake. "Everything is going perfect. All good," he repeated in self-talk. It was a relaxation technique he'd learned from one of his guests on the show at CNTV. All he had to do was think of something serene, pleasant, tranquil. *Think the color blue*, he said to himself, his eyelids drooping down over his pupils. *Bring the breathing down, heart rate too.* He knew his blood pressure would follow. A slight pain in his chest, the pain he felt now, was normal. He decided he wouldn't allow it to bother him.

"Are you okay, Mister Robertson?" Maria asked gently, entering the room with a new sense of urgency.

"What's all the flap about? And what's that for?" he demanded sternly, pointing to the wheel chair positioned ominously at the open door.

"I'll need to take you in for immediate observation. Doctor Peterson ordered the chair after reviewing your EKG."

"That bad?" He grinned, hoping to dispel the somber expression on Maria's face.

No response.

She helped him with his shirt and then pulled up the chair, pointing for him to be seated.

"Maria, really. I'm fine. I walked in here you know - "

"And I want you to walk out of here," she countered sternly. "Now sit."

There was no arguing. "You know, I've got a very important engagement tonight," he reminded her.

She answered him with a worried expression and a nod of the head.

"I'm feeling fine, really," Sam restated, an attempt to reassure her, and himself.

"Doctor Peterson will be right in. Relax now," she replied, tone more relaxed. "I'll be right back."

Sam knew what this meant. But he wasn't going to give in easily. Tonight was far too important to him.

5

GOOD OMEN

"Did I hear you use curse words just now, Mister Robertson?" Maria asked as she began hooking Sam up to the telemetry heart monitor.

"You sure did. Is this really necessary?"

"Doctor's orders."

"How about patient's rights? When am I going to see Doc Petersen, anyway?"

"He'd like you to rest, allow us to do this exam under conditions of observation. Then he'll be in to tell you what's going on. Come on, now," she said in her most motherly voice as she fluffed the pillows behind his head. "Let's not get your blood pressure up over this. It's for your own good."

"For my own good..." he mumbled like a toddler surrendering to a grownup.

"Just press this button by the bed if you need me. Here's the television controls, if you want to watch TV. I'll be back every few minutes to check on you."

Sam just waved her off as she exited the private single-bed hospital room. He was angry and resentful. He should have waited for these tests until after his second honeymoon trip was over. He didn't dare call Rachel to alarm her. He was determined to see Doc Peterson, get some answers, and walk out of there today. He'd had bypass surgery once and was warned that if he didn't stop smoking and drinking, he'd be digging an early grave for himself. He amazed himself by quitting cold turkey, a little more than one year ago, right after meeting Rachel. No more smokes, no more drinks.

He lay back, his stare burning a hole in the white acoustic tile ceiling, grappling for a way out, a way to make all this go away. He needed to find a way to improve his biological aging; his health. He needed Rachel. More than he could explain, he needed her and loved her. The patterned acoustic ceiling tile didn't respond.

If he *was* given a second chance, just one more decade to experience Rachel's love deeply and completely, he might be willing to bargain with God - show up in church - give up Sunday sports.

That was big of me, he chuckled cheerlessly to himself. *God, if there is a God, I'll regularly grace the threshold of your house if you will give me more time with Rachel.*

He pondered for a moment on the emptiness of that kind of prayer. Yet that is what he was willing to offer. He would sacrifice his one day of golf, hunting, fishing, NFL games, even his single glass of dinner wine... What else was there? Sam's mournful petition was suddenly interrupted by a familiar voice; clinical and anything but soothing.

"Sam, how are you feeling?" asked Doctor Peterson, chart in hand.

"I'm feeling fine, thanks. But I'm not happy with all this." Sam's arm swept back and forth to take in the array of machines, tubes and medical paraphernalia.

"Sam, I'll shoot straight with you, but you need to shoot straight with me. You've been experiencing chest pain?"

"Gas, maybe. Acid reflux. A little heartburn. I have ulcers, you know."

"Tingling down your left arm, leg, feet, toes?"

"Maybe a tickle..."

"Out of breath over simple tasks?"

"I quit smoking. My lungs are adjusting, that's all."

"Somewhat faint, lightheaded, dizzy?"

"Well, I fell in love last year..."

"Okay," interrupted Doctor Petersen, ignoring his patient's casual attitude. He squinted down at his chart. "I've got some bad news and good news. Which do you want first?"

Sam breathed out through pursed lips. "Give me the good."

"You're alive."

"Oh."

"You're alive and there's hope for a number of years yet in that overused heart of yours. Is that better?"

"The bad news?" Sam asked dejectedly.

"You need immediate bypass surgery."

"I just had bypass surgery when... a couple of years ago—remember?"

"That's right. But you need it again. Quadruple bypass, this time, Sam."

"You're sure?"

"Sam, I've seen this movie a thousand times. Your blood flow is severely restricted, here, here and here." His index finger wandered across Sam's chest and down his left arm. He pulled up a stool and sat next to the bed. "You must listen to me, now. I've known people with the symptoms you have who died before they were able to get through the door of this building. But the treadmill tests aren't always completely accurate. Just to make sure, I've ordered for an immediate angiogram."

"I hate those things. Can't you just x-ray me or something?" Sam pleaded. "A full-body scan with one of those new fancy do-everything, painless, see-it-all machines?"

"I need more information, if we're going to open you up again. I need to slide a catheter in, shoot dye into the veins, take a picture of your main coronary arteries. At minimum, you need to stay overnight for observation before we make the final decision."

Sam lay in heavy silence as the doctor observed the heart monitor he was hooked up to. Then, finally, he spoke up. "How serious is it?"

Doctor Peterson pointed at the jagged blips on the screen, as if dusting the front of the EKG machine with the tip of his finger. "See this line here? The rhythm of your heart is this line. You are heartbeats away from it going flat. That's how serious I believe it is."

"Ah, hell, Doc," sighed Sam. "There's got to be another way. How 'bout aspirin?"

Doctor Petersen didn't respond.

"There's got to be another way," Sam pled again.

"The other way is a bed sheet pulled up over your head."

"You don't need to be so callously truthful."

"So, if you'll sign this form, we'll get started."

Sam glanced over the authorization form, detailing a number of tests and possible surgery, then handed it back, saying, "No, thanks."

"What do you mean?" Doctor Petersen snapped in a clearly annoyed tone of voice.

"I mean I'm not going through with it...not for a week, anyway."

"You have a death-wish or something?"

"No, I want to live. Really live. I have a date with my wife tonight and a week in the Bahamas planned. I'm no worse today than I was last month, and the month before that. I'll be careful and be back in a week."

"I can't agree with that decision, Sam. Listen, this is me. I'm more than your doctor. We golf together, remember? We've been hell-raising together, two guys out on the town during our single days. This is Tom Petersen talking now. I can't, in good conscience, let you off the hook this easy."

"It's my decision to make. You won't be held responsible if anything happens to me."

"Okay, Sam. But as a professional, your leaving this hospital today will be under official protest. I'll have to ask you to fill out an AMA form."

"What's an AMA form?"

"A rarely-used document buried in our files somewhere. It's called an "Against Medical Advice" form. I need to make sure the evidence is clear that I performed my best medical observation, noting the advice given you from me, and your rejection of it. You're a stubborn man, Sam." He shook his head. "But it's your call."

"Send Maria in with the form. I'll sign it and be back next week. Go ahead and schedule me for a week from tomorrow."

"Sam, go easy on yourself on this trip. You know what I mean. Keep your excitement level balanced, avoid the rich foods, no smoking, drinking."

Sam's face elicited a smirk. "Excitement level down. Fat chance."

Doctor Petersen offered his hand. "Good luck, Sam," he said, brushing off his friend's nonchalance with another shake of the head.

"Hey, you act like it's over with me or something. Don't worry."

The doctor said nothing as he turned and left the room.

"Mister Robertson, I've been told you're being released. Your clothes are in the closet here. When you're ready, I'll need your signature on this form." She laid it on a tray next to the bed. "Then you're free to go."

"Thank you, Maria. You know, I like you. I'll be back next week with something special from the Bahamas for you." He shot her his most confident smile.

"You just be sure to come back standing up," she warned, wagging her finger at him. "That'll be good enough for me."

"What a God-forsaken, lousy mood these people are in," Sam mumbled as he slipped his trousers on.

Minutes later, standing outside, a crisp winter chill greeted him. Maybe *I can put this off until spring. I'll take the week off for Easter; let them cut me open. Then I'll come out a new man. And besides,* he considered, *Easter is a time of resurrection. A good omen,* he thought as he hailed a cab for his rendezvous with Rachel.

6

ARMS OF JESUS

"Hello, babe." Sam greeted her with a tender kiss. "You look marvelous, dear...*absolutely ma'velous*," he whispered, stealing a cue from his friend, comedian Billy Crystal.

"Thank you, Sam. Why the fancy duds?" Rachel asked, smiling as she ran her slender fingers down the lapel of his suit coat.

"I just want to look my best for you. Tonight's special; this whole week is special. I had these fitted by Alexander's down on Seventh Avenue."

"Suspenders and all?" she grinned. "What would Larry say?" she asked smiling.

"Suspenders and bow tie and all. I always wanted to be Larry when I grew up. Come on. I've got our table reserved." He slipped a 50-dollar bill into a waiter's palm and they followed him to a private corner, a table situated next to a gas-lit flame glowing in a hearthstone fireplace.

"This turn-of-the-century fireplace is all that's left of the original building," Sam observed as they were seated. "Did you know it was a bar where the mob - gangsters from the 1920s and '30s – hung out?"

Rachel, obviously impressed, nodded and beamed back at him. "So, how did the physical go today?" she asked casually.

"Movie stars, police commissioners and government officials on the take, all made this place the bar of choice," Sam pressed on. "The Irish mob had it for a few years, then the Italians moved in. Pretty interesting stuff."

Rachel, however, wouldn't be deterred. "So," she tried again, "what did the doc say?"

"*I'm gonna get dat bunny wabbit if its da wast fing I do*," he replied with a grin. "You know. Bugs Bunny? *Eh... What's up Doc?*" he imitated. "The guy with the shotgun pointing it down the bunny hole?"

"Sam?" she protested.

"Healthy as an ox," he answered, hoping she wouldn't pursue it further.

"What kind of an ox?" she laughed good-naturedly.

"More a bull than ox... Yeah. Like a raging, out-of-control Pamplona bull," he added, using his fingers to imitate horns.

"Sounds dangerous," she smiled as the waiter handed her a menu.

If you only knew, he thought to himself.

They ordered. All the while she eyed him suspiciously. Perhaps she detected some uncertainty in his facial expression or his posture. *Indeed,* he thought, *I'm hiding behind a façade.*

A minute or two passed – he wasn't sure. Then suddenly she stated matter-of-factly, "Something's wrong."

"Nothing's wrong," came the cavalier reply, eyes traveling the menu in an attempt to hide the truth.

Rachel reached across the candle-lit table and put her hand in his. "Remember the night we met, at the party?"

"Of course."

"I thought I was fulfilled, totally content – inside, I mean. I had my son, a good job, and God. But not a man. You made me feel whole."

Sam reddened with embarrassment. The window to his soul was broken as a solitary drop of moisture appeared a the corner of each eye. No woman had ever before said to him anything close to that.

"And you make me feel whole." His words came out stilted; forced.

Thought filled the silent void as they held hands, gently rubbing fingers together, smiling at one another, seeming to sense that the other had more on his or her mind than words could account for.

"There is one thing that bothers me though," Rachel added tenderly, after a moment more of the awkward stillness.

"What's that?" Sam asked, searching stunning azure eyes.

She hesitated, then simply stated the thing that troubled her. "You're *not* whole, *not* complete, and I don't know how to make it better."

"What do you mean? I'm happier than I've ever been in my entire life. You've brought me so much happiness. I've never been more whole..."

"Empty," she insisted.

"Rachel, what are you saying?" he asked emphatically. He leaned forward in his chair and jutted his face so close to the center-piece candle that it felt at least as hot as the sudden stirrings of frustration roiling inside him.

"Can you honestly say you feel one hundred percent complete? Or do you sense something's missing?"

"Okay, Rachel, I surrender. Tell me what I'm missing," he challenged, slumping back in his seat.

"Sam, I want your happiness. I also look at what you've done for me, for Michael, and how hard you try to be better in every way. I love your generosity, the kindness you show, your humor, and I think you're handsome. It isn't hard to be in love with you, but it is hard knowing something about wholeness and not knowing how to convey it to you in a way that you will embrace, accept."

"Go on, Rachel. I'm listening."

"When I was nine years old, I came down with Scarlet Fever. As you know, it can turn into a life-threatening illness, permanently damage the heart. And that's exactly what happened. Within days, I was at St. Jude's in Memphis, fighting for my life. There were many prayers said for me.

"My father and mother were constantly at my bedside and I felt somehow safe. I told them I knew Jesus would make me better and not to worry. I knew if they were there, praying for and with me, that everything would be alright.

"But one night something wonderful began to happen. My father was there at my bedside asleep. I thought I was calling out to him, frightened at first, by this strange feeling inside of me. Then I became very warm, happy, and free from pain and illness.

"I felt myself leave my bed, light as a feather. I was walking toward a bright but happy glow. It was the warmest sensation, far warmer than sunlight feels, but it didn't burn. My entire insides tingled with excitement; I felt wonderful. The light soon gathered around a man standing there, and I knew who it was, instinctively.

"He reached his hand out to me and I took it, totally unafraid and willing to be with him. We sat down on a stone-type bench beside a fountain in the middle of the prettiest meadow, with so many different kinds of flowers. The colors were incredible. Then Jesus asked me, '*How do you feel?*' as he cradled me in his arms. "I feel whole again, like I'm home," my innocent thoughts answered back.

"'*Little one*,' he said, '*your faith has made you whole*,' then he kissed me and walked me back toward the same light. I didn't want to go back, but realized I must.

"The next thing I knew I was in my bed, crying, with nurses and a doctor milling around, all concerned, giving me oxygen. One of the nurses was listening for my heartbeat, and my parents were crying. They leaned down and hugged me when I coughed a breath of air.

"The next day, a doctor came to my room and was going down a checklist with my parents, marveling at the turnaround in my health, and said, 'Looks like we've cured her. You can take her home now.'

"You didn't cure me..." I remember blurting out. They all smiled and we went home. Later, I told my parents about the experience and they believed me, but nothing more was ever made of it.

"Sam, from that day on, I've never feared death. My childlike faith had made me 'whole,' but the love I felt with the man in my dream was real to me, and still is."

Sam's mind was reeling. "I wish I could believe like that," he responded simply. "Why haven't you shared this with me before?"

"Some things are too personal. I've learned that just because one person has a sacred experience, that doesn't necessarily mean that others will believe it or be affected by it. I've been ridiculed for my faith in the past, so I try not to wear it on my sleeve. I just quietly live it. That's something I want you to have...faith, I mean. But I don't know how to - " She paused as she searched for the way to finish her thought. Sam leaned back in his chair, his lips tightening into a forced smile. "What's wrong?" Rachel asked.

"Nothing's wrong. Nothing at all. Here comes the food," he beamed and rubbed his hands together. "I love you, Rachel. Promise you won't give up on me."

"I promise."

7

REGRETS

The screeching, pneumatic wail of the ambulance siren sent taxis jostling to the sides of the busy intersection, clearing a narrow path as they rushed him to New York City Hospital. Rachel sat in the back, holding Sam's hand as he fought the crushing pain in his chest.

"I love you, sweetheart," she offered tearfully, kissing the tip of his middle knuckle while trying to avoid getting in the way of the two EMT's hunched over him on each side.

He nodded bravely, seeking a way to tell her he'd make it, that he'd be okay if she would just stay by him. The EMT's rushed him into the emergency room. The ER staff bustled to his side, stabilizing him before prepping him for the immediate surgery.

"Mrs. Robertson?"

"Yes?"

"My name is Tom Petersen. I'm a friend of Sam's and his personal physician," he said, reaching out his hand to greet her.

"Oh! Thank you for coming!" She dabbed at the puffiness that had formed around her eyes. "I've heard good things about you from Sam."

"Well, I've tried to stay on his good side. Naturally, you must know of my concern for his condition."

"Of course," she replied, gaining more composure. "Will he be...alright?" she asked.

"That's what I came down to talk to you about. Please, take a seat in here..." He guided her gently by the arm to an empty clerk's room off the waiting area.

"So – are they going to perform surgery right away?"

"They're prepping him as we speak."

"Will you do the surgery?"

"No. I've asked a friend, a highly trained specialist to take charge. But I'll be in the operating room, right there by his side. There's something else going on I need to let you know about. It complicates this a bit."

Rachel appeared momentarily confused, gesturing for him to continue with a nod of the head.

"He's bleeding profusely. It looks as though it's been going on in a mild form for some time. He has stomach ulcers, but it wasn't detected this morning in exams. This is sudden and massive. We'll be doing two surgeries before this is over. Right now, he's receiving a blood transfusion."

"He's tough," she reassured herself, nodding at her own whispered affirmation.

"Yes, he is. That's making the difference right now," agreed the physician. "In any case, I thought you should know. I'll be there the entire time."

"I appreciate that so much," she replied, feigning a smile. She paused to gather her emotions, then continued. "What kind of chance - I mean, what are his chances? I think you have a percent figure in cases like this?"

"Yes. I would put it at 50/50 right now. He's in extremely critical condition. I guess he told you he waived the advice I gave him this morning?"

"No. I don't understand. What do you mean 'waived'?" she asked, clearly perplexed by the statement.

"Sam signed a form stating that he understood he was rejecting my advice that he be admitted immediately for possible bypass surgery. Frankly, I don't know how he lasted so long in his present condition. Most men die from these kinds of cardiac arrests. He has a very strong will to live."

"I still don't understand." Her head wagged in numb disbelief, her voice crackling with emotion. "I hear what you just said about the waiver, but I don't understand why Sam wouldn't take your advice... He's not stupid. Why would he do this?" Her reddened eyes, now swimming in tears, posed the same question her voice just had. "You couldn't force him?"

"No. Force is not something we can do. And no one forces Sam on anything, anyway. I learned that long ago."

"I feel lost. I don't know what to do," Rachel squeaked out as she trembled, finally breaking down.

Doctor Peterson pulled up his chair alongside hers and offered his arm. "He's alive because of you, Rachel. You are the reason he'll pull through this. If you believe in miracles, it's a good time to pray for one. Can you do that? I can send the hospital's chaplain in to visit with you, if you like."

Rachel patted his arm. "No, that's fine. I'll be okay. I do believe. It will turn out according to God's will," she sniffled. "Thank you. I feel better talking to you. Is there another waiting area closer to the operating room?"

He nodded. "I'll take you there. I promise to keep you fully informed during the next couple of hours." He gestured towards the door. "Shall we?"

For the next several hours, Rachel's mind swam in a blur of emotions. Then it finally settled on the blustering Sam, so filled with answers, so filled with life. She'd come to love him deeply. At last her mind turned to a recent argument, one she wished they hadn't had.

***

"How can you know? I mean, you haven't seen this Jesus you so adamantly argue is the *real* deal..."

"Don't you even believe he lived?"

"I'm not that stupid," he huffed. "Of course I believe he lived. The circumstantial evidence is overwhelming." They were standing in the kitchen, she cooking Sunday dinner and he having just arrived to invite her to go out; to leave, just spend the Sunday on a drive, alone – and not attend another Sunday Worship meeting, six months straight now without a miss.

"It's practically my only day off," he pled.

"Is that my fault? You knew this about me when you married me. Maybe you should work less."

"Look, if God exists, he's not going to strike us down for missing a day at church here or there."

"What do you mean by '...missing a day here or there'? You've been all of two times in six months."

Sam scoffed. "I don't want to get the man upstairs too used to seeing me there. I wouldn't want to put him or anyone else into a state of shock..."

"You are so sacrilegious!" she fumed.

"No, I'm just not so sacrosanct. I just don't happen to believe..." he cut his remark short, inserting in its place his favorite expletive.

"You don't need to swear!" she responded angrily.

He rolled his eyes in exasperation.

"Look," she said, teary-eyed, spatula in hand, "...maybe you don't believe, but that doesn't mean it isn't so. He, Jesus, is testified of and witnessed and praised by more people through history than any other man...including you!"

Sam shrugged at the last jab. "He's *referred* to more than any other man of his time period and generation, I grant you that. But so much has been done in this Jesus' name. Wars fought, crusades waged, lives taken. What kind of God is that?"

Sam sought a more calm, conciliatory tone. "Look, Rachel, I need evidence. You can't just wander around believing in someone who's been dead for two thousand years just because a bunch of fanatical followers make a bunch of strident claims about his magical powers."

"There was a book written, you know," she countered. "A bestseller year after year for several centuries now. What do you think of that, Sam? Your only book made it to the bestseller list for, what, two weeks? You can't fool me, Sam. I know you've been reading the scriptures I gave you for Christmas when I'm away at church... Alone!"

"I have a healthy curiosity, yes. I'm not totally cold, unwilling to be convinced. It's just that, for me, I can believe in God in a number of ways. Out in nature, for example. Out there I see a greater design. I actually think about the possibility of God when I go hunting or fishing with my brothers."

Sam realized he'd touched a deep nerve in Rachel as soon as the words had tumbled from his lips. Stammering, he began to backtrack, apologize, looking for a way to take back what he'd said.

"Listen, Sam," Rachel tearfully said, pointing directly at him now. "My first husband used to say that same thing to me all the time and - "

Sam interrupted her, "I know, babe," he said softly, gently, approaching her to stroke her face, her arms. "I'm sorry. I know. I didn't mean..."

"You hear me out," she muttered, pulling away from him. "It's funny how many men go hunting for God - with a gun - fishing for truth - with a rod and reel in hand. Michael Sr. was killed on an iced-over highway in Wyoming out 'hunting for God,' while I was home taking our little boy to church. You have no idea how let down I felt by that," tearfully adding, "I won't buy into that macho nonsense again!"

**

That had been nearly six months ago now. He was a good man, a kind man. He had more belief than he really understood.

If only, she thought. *If only some greater power could intercede, give him the chance he needed to see* - and give her just a little more time with him. If his heart could be made whole, be healed. She closed her eyes in prayer, bowing her head right there in the neon-lit office. She made promises; she bargained with God to let him live, even if it was a few years more.

Now, with nothing more she could do, she folded her arms on the cold desk in front of her, laid her head down and let her exhausted mind give way to the slumber she so desperately needed. No matter what happened, she would stay with him, right to the end.

8

NEAR DEATH

Sam, somewhere in the fog of semi-consciousness, was aware that he was being prepped for surgery, but unable and too weak to offer many words of thanks to those working to save his life.

Sedated, he felt he was drifting. He knew the feeling from his past surgery. The pain in his chest had diminished and he felt relaxed, though hooked up to respirators and monitored carefully by the intensive care unit nurses.

His pupils contracted in response to the overhead lamps directly above his head. He could feel his arms being extended and strapped down to the germ-free stainless steel fold-out sleeves of the operating table, as if positioning him in a T-like human-size crucifix, his arms stretched wide for whatever was to come.

Strange...he could make out the face of the nurse speaking to him, patting him so gently, as if he were dying. He saw her sympathetic face reassuring him from above. "I'm Janean," she articulated in a way that made it seem that her patient spoke some sort of foreign tongue. "I'll be right here with you. You'll be fine, Mister Robertson. I promise, I will be right here," she was saying.

He mouthed a slurred reply, now that the anesthetic was taking full effect. "My older sister's name is Janean," he mumbled. "Gone. Gone a long time," he ended. He could see the nurse's lips moving, hear the muffled sounds of other voices, but now he felt at peace, relaxed, totally submissive, as his eyes, heavy from drugs, willingly surrendered to the coming darkness.

***

"Who are you?" he asked the large man in the white robe walking him down the corridor to the elevator.

No answer, just a smile.

"How did my surgery go? Must have gone well... I'm feeling great," he chuckled, mostly to himself, as they passed through the open door.

"So, we going to post-op? Checking out, maybe?" Sam's questions rolled from his lips as they strode briskly down the long, brightly lit, antiseptically clean corridor.

The big man, his escort, replied with a courteous smile, "I'm sure you will find your accommodations acceptable and the company agreeable."

Sam felt comfortable. No reason not to. The operation had been a breeze and he was feeling like a million bucks, ready to go on that anniversary trip with Rachel. He wondered where she was.

"Your wife is a good woman, Samuel," his host noted as the elevator doors slid open. "She has been praying for you." The tall, athletic-looking man ushered Sam out of the elevator into a lush garden landscape filled with more varieties of gloriously painted flowers and shrubs than Sam had ever seen in one place.

"Wow!" he offered in a reverent and spontaneous childlike refrain. "They usually give me the best room in the hospital – the best view – but this? Why haven't I seen it before?" he mumbled, awed by his new surroundings.

The large man backed his way into the elevator. "Make yourself at home, Samuel," he called.

Sam nodded, lost in the utter magnificence of the place. Nearby, a fountain burbled from a clear pool, sending a fine mist of water into the sky, creating an arcing rainbow and scattering dew-like droplets upon ferns, flowers, and the lower, spongy groundcover, the waters finally collecting to form a gently flowing rivulet that led off into a distant field of gray.

"Where does it lead?" Sam found himself asking no one.

"Why don't you find out?" he heard the voice, more distant now, as he turned to face it.

"Hello! Sir? Hello?" He poked his head around the courtyard-oasis, peering back over his shoulder in search of the hospital elevator. A forest wall of well-manicured willows, aspen, fir, and elegantly trimmed but leafy shrubs of every emerald tint greeted him. "Hello? Anyone?"

Mingling with the forest green were carpets of lawn and scattered among the flora, obvious to even the most untrained eye, grew exquisitely cared-for orchids of every color and variety, their heavy heads bowing as if to give homage to a master gardener. Sam found himself in deep admiration for them as he caressed the velvety petals. "Bird of Paradise. Rachel's favorite," he admired.

The mixed scents of flower and leaf seemed to soothe Sam's mind. He lingered there at the edge of the pool, momentarily forgetting the man who had brought him here.

He had to find Rachel. She simply had to see this place. The Hospital Board of Governors were to be congratulated. That would be the first thing he would do when he was released, congratulate them for creating this marvelous healing environment. Then he'd have Mary Kelly, his show's producer, invite them on, explain how all this aided in the healing process.

No doubt he was the first guest to see it. They were trying to make an impression on him. That was it. Sure. He was an important figure in the media. It would go a long way in their efforts to gain notoriety for this new remodel if, on his show, he made mention of their rehabilitation garden. Now everything was coming together. Except...

He turned suddenly. A new vista opened up to his view. The crystal-clear streamlet, once so full and babbling, now had run almost dry. What water remained, seemed to flow through an arid desert. *What's all this?* his mind silently posed.

"A place where you may forever quench your thirst," he heard the voice answer, now coming from some distance ahead of him.

"Such a pleasant voice," he muttered, "but not real." He ambled along one side of the crystalline brook, stopping betimes to scoop some of the tempting moisture into his hands, letting it trickle through his fingers. *Like liquefied diamond.* Sam brought some to his lips. Sweet, satisfying, cool. "Forever quench my thirst," he said aloud, conscious of the meanderings of his medically sedated mind.

The hospital had really performed a miracle, he thought. *Good idea. Walls with scenes so real... No one could get hurt trying to leave. Why would they want to?* His mind wandered to explore a thousand other possibilities. *It could be a dream.*

All his worries seemed a million miles away right now. The anesthesiologist was to be congratulated. It really, really had made him relaxed. *As a matter of fact, it felt so good, he should have surgery more often.* Sam chuckled at the thought. *This is a splendid dream,* he decided.

He wondered if he would awaken soon. He really didn't mind this at all. *This is way better than the Bahamas,* he silently mused, pleased at the incisive yet serene powers his mind had assumed.

Check in here with Rachel. That would be nice, he thought, smiling, and now talking to himself in a normal, everyday tone of voice. *Time to wake up now, Sam,* he reminded himself as he continued to follow the brook, winding its way into a ravine. It surprised him to come to its end. A bone-dry stretch of sand now paralleled the streamlet until it swallowed it entirely, the hollow of its bed disappearing into the foot of a forbiddingly steep knoll, devoid of vegetation.

A hill? How did they do that? he marveled, kicking at the sandy mixture with... *Sandals? Leather sandals... Hmm.* He reached down to stroke their soft straps. His body felt no pain whatsoever; in fact, he was as strong and vibrant as ever. Mystified, he marveled at his rapid recovery from surgery.

He inspected the fine quality of his hospital gown, his hands caressing the satiny...*toga?* He spun around to look for the garden he had just come from. *Gone!* "Where in the..." he muttered. "Am I...?"

Nothing but desolation for as far as his eyes could see. It was as if he had entered another dimension, some sort of dreamed-up, sci-fi flick of the mind caused, he guessed, by the drugs he'd been administered. At any moment he expected the famed black-and-white '60s *Twilight Zone* TV series host Rod Serling to appear. *I really gotta wake up now,* he implored.

Dead...the real-life characters of so many of the television shows he'd enjoyed as a youth, had already passed beyond the vast unknown into that other dimension, only to find they were really... *Uh oh...*

Something – an inner doubt, a change of scenery? – had suddenly shattered the serene, familiar feeling that had enveloped him just moments before. Now he was caught in a whirlpool of panic; an out-of-control state-of-being that rarely, if ever, he'd sensed before. In real life, Sam Robertson was always in control.

This sudden abandonment into a hellish landscape brought about a terror beyond any he could imagine with his waking mind. The realization that he was being played with, though, spurred Sam to force thoughts into his brain designed to calm himself, help him find a level of equilibrium, understand the situation so he could manage it. He felt the tingle of something running across his foot and instinctively reached down to scratch at it. What, of the countless possibilities, could it be this time?

"God help me!" he screamed, kicking violently at the fist-size scorpion that had taken a defensive posture next to his instep. "Help me, God! Get me out of here! Somebody. Anybody! What's going on?" He turned and scuttled headlong in the direction from which he had come.

A few hurried strides brought him face to face with the awfulness of his predicament: before him lay nothing but sand, miles and miles of desert wasteland.

His racing heart skipped a beat. *I must be alive. I feel it pounding like it did when I ran for my life ten years ago in Pamplona to feel the rush Hemingway had described.* When a mad, raging bull charges at you, Sam knew, it's the experience of a lifetime. On that occasion, at least, its horns had found another adventurer instead.

He glanced about for an answer. Suddenly, he was short of breath. Bent over to recover, at last he looked up. There the hill rose up once more in front of him, filling the horizon, and a strange noise was coming from somewhere beyond it. He hadn't heard it 'til now. *Children laughing. People. Other patients*, he assured himself.

Anxious to solve the riddle of his baffling surroundings, Sam scuttled up the steep rise. Reaching its crest, he came upon a small cluster of brick dwellings, clean and whitewashed but definitely third-world style. Desert homes, these were situated in a depression that ran between this hill and two others beyond. On either side a road led from the village to a higher elevation, barren with just low-lying spring grasses and dry shrubs, rolling, California-type foothills spanning the eastern and western horizons.

I'm losing my mind. This stuff they put me to sleep with... No, it's gotta be a dream. Just a dream. I'm hot, and perspiring - thirsty, too. Can that happen in a dream?

His mind answered its own interrogatory. *Yes, that can all happen in a dream.*

He stumbled as he jogged down the gentle slope, falling hands first, scratching and peeling the skin on his palms. They bled! He sat up, stunned, checking himself out, unsure of his new world...who he was...where he was...what was happening.

Seemingly, from out of nowhere, the rough, calloused grip of a strong construction-type – the kind of hand accustomed to hard, manual labor – reached down and lifted him up by his shoulders. "You!" Sam cried out when he turned to see his rescuer. "It's you! What is this, some kind of joke? You escorted me to a garden, at the hospital, and now this?"

The strapping man held up his hand as if to slow Sam down. "You are alive, are you not?" the resonating voice asked.

"If this is a dream, it is the most vivid one I've ever had. I was in heaven one minute and the next in – "

"Hell?"

"Yeah!"

The man smiled. "You are Samuel Robertson, the famous personality who conducts television interviews?"

Sam nodded.

"Here, let me cleanse those wounds for you." The congenial fellow then picked up a dried gourd with a hole in the top and tilted it above Sam's scraped hands. From the gourd flowed a startlingly steady stream of water, bathing his hands in its cool, soothing wetness. The man then gently dried them on the sash of his own immaculate robe.

"Am I dead?" By this time Sam had every reason to wonder. Perhaps his spirit had slipped from his body without him realizing it? And this angel-like being...what about him? He possessed so much knowledge about Sam. Could he be some sort of guardian angel? On his program, Sam had interviewed guests who claimed to have had NDE's – "near death experiences" – but could he, himself, now be experiencing one?

"I am dead, right?" he asked again.

"Look around you. What do you see?" his host answered as he began now cleansing Sam's feet with the same water-filled gourd, drying them with the same robe.

Sam scanned the area once more, trying to see something; anything else that he'd overlooked before. "I see an ancient-looking village of dried mud-brick homes, a few palm trees, some goats, a couple of children playing... I'm in the Middle East. Probably some poor country, like Yemen, where time has stood still for two thousand years."

"Very perceptive. Yet time, as you know it, doesn't stand still, Samuel," the man said kindly, as if instructing a child. "It is always *present*. Yes, you are indeed in the Middle East. And you are standing in a village that is very much two thousand years old yet, also very much alive, as it was then. You are in Emmaus, and but a half-day's journey up that road is Jerusalem."

"Wait. Hold on. We walk down the hospital corridor, enter an elevator, and it opens into this courtyard and garden. And now I've gone back in time to the land of Israel in the year..."

The strong voice added the year and then said, "It's the 7th day and the first month of Nisan in the Jewish calendar. Yes. The past is very much alive. And you have been given a chance to experience it for a very special reason. You have a broken heart, Samuel. But it is broken for the wrong reasons. It must be mended and you must make a final *Sam Robertson Report* in order for it to happen."

Sam's face registered a mixture of confusion and frustration. "What do you mean?"

"You are sad. Your heart is diseased. You wish to live longer than what your heart should allow. You wish this because of love—for the joy of living with your beloved Rachel. No?"

"Yes..." Sam stammered. "But how do you know all this?" He stared directly up into the congenial, sympathetic face of his host, genuinely seeking an answer.

"I am known as '*the friend*' to those I serve. I want you to look over there." The man pointed off into the distance.

"Okay," Sam replied, his gaze following the flight of the man's outstretched arm. "I'm looking. Now what?" He turned to face the man, but he was no longer there; it was if he'd vanished in thin air "Hello? Hey! This isn't funny anymore!"

Once again he turned in the direction the man had pointed. There before him, just down the hill and skirting the road, now stood the largest of the white-washed structures. And suddenly, flashing into his mind as though on a Times Square marquee, came the distinct words—more an impression, than anything: *Seek for one*

Cleopas, husband of Mary, a disciple and one of those called to assist the twelve. Grant him an interview, and also his request. And you may yet live.

Sam shook his head, hoping to dislodge the cobweb of sleep or dream or drug-induced vision that had infiltrated his head. Clearly, he was in some sort of science-fiction nether-zone-come-true, in another place, not in a hospital recovery room.

Others enter the garden and stay, the same voice abruptly whispered to him. Sam bolted, turned, expecting to see him; the large man, his guide. *Do your report, and you shall have both what your heart requires and what your heart longs for.*

Sam looked down at the blanket of sand that lay beneath his feet. When he nudged at it with the toe of his sandal, several grains flicked up and lodged between his toes. Reaching down to brush the sand away, he now became aware of his hands and, bringing them to his face, he mopped away the moisture beading on his brow. It was then, in that very moment, he determined to see this through and do as the stranger – this 'friend' – would ask. Whatever he was experiencing, be it hallucination or dream, he had no choice but to go through it and not around it.

9

CLEOPAS OF EMMAUS

"Hello! Anyone home?" Sam knocked on the rough-hewn cedar door. It creaked open. "Hello?"

"Shalom, stranger. What brings a Roman nobleman to our tiny village on this Sabbath evening?" a shallow but husky voice called out from deep within the eerily empty room.

The drawn face of a large, middle-aged bearded man greeted Sam from a darkened corner of the cavern-like room. Lit only by the faint glow of a candle on one end of an innkeeper's table and the glowing embers from a smoldering fire in the stone hearth, the diffused rays of light from the dancing flames caused a shadow to leap from the man. A giant apparition, the image spread across the wall and ceiling before him.

Sam figured he might as well play along with whatever experience he was having. Recalling the name given him moments before, he blurted out, "I seek one called Cleopas. Do you know him?"

"I am Cleopas of Emmaus," the man answered glumly. "What brings a Roman, such as you, sir, to our humble inn on the Sabbath?"

"You call me Roman. Is it apparent?" answered Sam, glancing down at his fine linen toga.

"Ha! You are playing with my mind. Please, sir, I am far too tired for that."

Sam just nodded. *Strange place... man... dream.* He decided to push the experience along, since it wouldn't disappear on its own. "I have come to learn something of you," he found himself saying.

"You speak Aramaic well," answered Cleopas as he arose to greet Sam formally. "A Roman, come to learn something of a Jew, at a lowly trading route inn? But then again, you wouldn't be the first. An innkeeper hears many strange things from guests. You are a detective of the court, of course. Are you not?"

"Detective? No. I want to know what's going on, you know, here in..."

"Emmaus? This village? Nothing happens in Emmaus. But Jerusalem? That is another matter."

"Yes. So answer me...let's get this dream out of the way. Tell me about the man they called Jesus of Nazareth. He lived here long ago, yes?" Sam asked, unaware that he was speaking anything but his Jersey-born English. He pawed at the sash wrapped about his waist and found a leather bag filled with coins and a rolled document of some sort.

"Dream! It is so...and a terrible one at that," the man stammered in reply. "Ha! A spy! You came here to deceive me!"

"Not a spy," Sam countered.

"Oh! So you, a Roman, are so utterly unaware, uneducated of matters in this land," the big man sarcastically rejoined.

"I have money...and this," Sam said holding the scroll out for the Hebrew to see.

"I do not need money to talk about the Master," Cleopas exclaimed, "but I am interested in that document." He lifted a hand to cradle it, unrolled it gently, and quickly perused it. "Written in Latin and Greek," he observed, "but not our tongue of Palestine. No matter. You will present this to only the most educated, I presume."

"Yes," Sam answered without hesitation.

"So you are Samuel Antonius, a nobleman of Sicilia, and a representative of the Library of the Senate in Rome?"

Sam, though his brain was spinning in uncertainty, offered the slightest nod. He had changed his last name to Robertson when he entered the News business. Somehow "Sam Anthony" just didn't carry like Robertson, his mother's maiden name. His mind was upon the angel mother now, long departed from life. *Strange dream, this is*, he mused.

"You are a member of the Antonius family of politicians, no doubt," Cleopas went on. "You are not *the* Senator Antonius, the one who supports so liberally the Sanhedrin treasury and Caiaphas, the Sadducee High Priest of the Temple?"

"No."

"Here is the seal of the Senator," Cleopas pressed.

"Yes, indeed. So it is," Sam replied. *Less is more,* he reminded himself. He knew enough to keep silent. *Besides this is a dream that will wander where it wants to go,* he assured his mind.

"Well, you must be the senator's ambassador, or his seal would not appear on this document," Cleopas muttered in self-talk, though loud enough for Sam to realize the role he would be playing in this drama within a drama: indeed, he would play the part of an observer.

"Just an interested citizen of the world, as the document claims. I am not at liberty to say more," Sam found himself saying.

"The Hebrew name Samuel given you; curious. Perhaps that would explain also the favors of the Senator to our Jewish High Priest and his clan. A shrewd man, naming his kinsmen for Hebrew prophets. It is said he plays Herod Antipas against the powerful High Priest. You are his brother, then? Kin, surely," Cleopas pressed, rising from his seat.

"I pay little attention to this Senator called Antonius and his dealings, nor do I wish to speak of him further," Sam adroitly countered. "All I can say at this time is that my journey has brought me from far across the sea. A man told me to come and seek you out. So I am here. Will you help me?"

Sam had exhausted his reasons for finding himself standing before this stranger who, seemingly, had stepped out of Cecil B. DeMille's *Ten Commandments.* He must carefully tailor his words to meet the situation. He would speak truthfully, but would be obliged to obscure who he really was. He only hoped the man would cease his inquisitive probing so this whole vision – this surgery-induced nightmare – might end.

Cleopas sized his guest up and down as he paced the floor, thoughtfully stroking his whiskered chin. Finally he pulled up short in front of Sam and stated, "I have nothing to lose by telling a respected Roman citizen what I know. I am already a lost man. If you are a spy of the judges of the Sanhedrin, so be it. If you are here on an errand of Procurator Pilate, so be it as well. I am a disciple and have nothing to hide.

"I was orphaned as a young lad by the fever sickness that swept our land in my eighth year," he continued. "When my parents died I was raised by an uncle in

Bethlehem, not far from here. It was there I first learned the innkeeper's trade. And it was there I lost my soul..." His voiced trailed off and his head bowed in a mixture hopeless anguish. After some time he resumed his story. "My wife's name is Mary, also one who has suffered great slander for being a disciple's wife - may God bless her name forever."

"Yes, may God bless her," Sam responded, surprising himself at his words. Then he peered around the room. "Can you tell me why things are so quiet?"

"You are a stranger indeed to Judea, or you continue your ruse," Cleopas muttered, shaking his head. "No matter. I will tell you. It is still the Sabbath. At the going down of the sun, the sixth hour, a caravan protected by a Roman Centurion, a man known for his kindness to the Jews and a sympathizer to our cause, will pass by. The roads are not safe for travelers who venture on their own after sundown.

"I leave for Jerusalem and there will abide with one called Simon. He is awaiting word from me on some important matters. I serve as a relay for messages being conveniently employed on this trade route to the sea. The Roman friend also carries messages and delivery as a favor for the brethren. I mustn't delay. If you wish to know more of my Master, you are welcome to travel with us then."

"*Simon?*" Sam slipped verbally at the shock of the sudden recognition. "Simon *Peter!*"

"Yes, Simon known also by the surname Cephas; Peter in the Greek tongue. You *are* a spy then," Cleopas scowled. "Do you not weary in your persecutions?"

Sam felt himself stiffen at this latest accusation. "I am no spy, sir," he repeated, the words issuing from his lungs in rather clipped, staccato bursts. Now he felt wholly engrossed in this dreamy drama.

"Certainly," Cleopas huffed, spurning the Gentile's attempt at a ruse. "By the way," he added, his tone turning sarcastic, "you came here alone, on foot from the coast?"

A lilting smile creased Sam's lips. "I had a special conveyance," he offered simply.

"You are a mysterious man, Samuel Antonius. You have hardly a soiled spot on your garments. To have walked far, it would be apparent, and you would have a day-sack or bag with you. But here you are, at my door, appearing from nowhere. Strange. Very strange, indeed – if, that is, you are not a spy."

"Indeed," Sam muttered under his breath. Then aloud for Cleopas to hear, "As you say, it is mysterious. I do my best work under those circumstances."

10

EN VINO VERITAS

"Well, mystery man or not, spy or no, you must be hungry sir," Cleopas noted, slightly less suspicious. "I have no fear of you now," he added, shaking his head in obvious sadness. Then, almost inaudibly, he muttered in self-condemning afterthought, "Would that I had gone myself..."

The innkeeper motioned Sam to take a spot near the fire's embers, still smoldering in the stone hearth. "I will have a healthy portion of Passover lamb served to you. Sariah?" he called out.

A young woman, perhaps eighteen years of age, appeared from the room behind the wall where the fire blazed. Modestly dressed, her loose-fitting gown gave her the appearance of an angel. She smiled and bowed respectfully, shyly, toward Cleopas's guest.

"Pleased to meet you," Sam offered.

"Shalom.... Peace be to you as well, sir," she answered.

"Daughter, this is Samuel Antonius of Rome. Will you please bring him something to eat, and our best wine, most recently pressed."

"Yes, father." Sariah nodded courteously and returned to what Sam presumed was a kitchen area.

"A fair child. Do you have other children?" Sam inquired.

"We had...but the sword of sickness took our only son from us when he was a tender-aged child of two years. I have a married daughter who lives in Bethany, and this girl, Sariah, the joy-song of my heart. She is betrothed to wed a Galilean later in the month, a young lad now living in Jerusalem. One named John Mark."

John Mark, he mused. "A Galilean? Wasn't Jesus, whom you call *Master*, a Galilean?"

Cleopas's countenance shifted with the ease of a feather carried on a gentle breeze. "He was a Galilean prophet, yes. But the early morning hours, day before yesterday, the High Priest Caiaphas and the Sanhedrin had Procurator Pilate question him. They accused him of treason, punishable by death. I could not be there to stand up for my Lord. No," he spat out in bitter self-loathing, "I was here at the inn, as usual, caring for my precious shekels and guests!"

"So did they – " Sam started.

"Execute him?" Cleopas asked with reddened eyes. "Crucify him?" he offered in rhetorical tone. "I have heard from returning guests that three men were executed. Some say he was. But I cannot believe it. No! I must not believe it until the Centurion reports it. From his own voice, then..."

"I am sorry Cleopas. I am against such capital punishment myself. Lock a man away, throw away the key if you must, but execution must be reserved for killers, murderers, not self-appointed teachers or Messiahs – "

"He was no self-appointed teacher!" Cleopas shot back. "Nor was he self-appointed to be Messiah! I, myself, heard from the very lips of a shepherd who, the night of the holy birth – the very night I turned the newborn Master into the cold.... I heard from Elias, a devout man not given to drink nor guile. He who guarded the temple flocks...those pure lambs bound for sacrifice! He and his hired herdsmen were given to hear the joyous sounds of heavenly choirs!"

Cleopas once more took to pacing the plank floor. Earnest, he expounded on the blessed event. "Yes, it was so! They heard angels sing! A shepherd, a mere boy, witnessed one of the angels descend from heaven! A lad, mind you – children do not lie! And there was the star. A sign in the heavens! No, you cannot understand. I do not condemn anyone for it. I cannot even describe it. So many witnesses... You are simply..."

"Uninformed?"

"Yes," Cleopas rejoined sullenly. "If they did execute him in your typical barbarous Roman fashion, then my dear sweet Mary, she must have..." He pressed his fingers to his weary eyes to squeeze at the moisture flooding them. "My Mary was there, residing in Bethany with the man's mother of the same name and one also of Magdala – a favored name for women so blessed to have been so loved and esteemed by our Master. My Mary is yet in Jerusalem and awaits me. She had more courage than I," he stammered. Then he pounded the table with his fist and looked up in hopes of finding solace from something unseen, to no avail. Tears came freely now as he strode the floor in anguish and fretted over some unspeakable, unfathomable incident.

Sam paused, taking it all in. He was angry at himself for not having listened to Rachel, for not having studied the Bible more. He knew the story, in general, but all these players in the drama, their names, their various roles...he was unsure how it all fit together. He couldn't ask the right questions without a script. And he always used a script in his interviews.

To Sam's relief, Cleopas raised his head and made the first move. "You know of the events of this past week, yesterday no doubt? I would be very surprised if you had not heard."

"I know of the feast called the Passover, which brings many thousands to Jerusalem, and I have heard tales of disturbances made by the man Jesus...a Zealot, I believe?"

Cleopas just stared at Sam in disbelief. Then he let out a laugh, followed by a sarcastic chuckle and a disdainful shake of the head. One last, peculiar mournful chortle issued from his chest, and he wiped at his sleep-deprived eyes, which still sought some sign from Sam, the merest hint, that he was playing him the fool.

"I am sorry, Samuel, my spying friend. You must try another profession," he mocked. "Oh, it is good to laugh," he added. "You must not think I am making you out to be a fool or that I am of a light heart because of my laughter. It is so strange to meet one as yourself. So Roman, yet if not a spy, then so innocent." He paused, his gaze still hovering over his guest. "Perhaps that is not the correct word. Why should I be surprised that, as a newcomer to this land, you are so poorly-versed."

"Father? Where shall I place the victuals?" the sweet voice of Sariah broke in.

Cleopas pointed to a spot on the rock hearth next to Sam. "And the wine. Don't forget a cup and a flask, sweet child."

"Yes, father." She set down the steaming wooden bowl and went to bring the cup and flask of freshly squeezed wine.

"Ignorant. You wanted to use the word *ignorant*," Sam offered with a smile. He examined the bowl of lamb, herbs and pita-style flat bread, wondering where to start.

"Eat. Eat," Cleopas urged, and with a chuckle added, "My heart has been heavy. You, somehow, have brought amusement to me. Like from another world..."

Sam raised his eyebrows as if to confirm the innkeeper's statement. "Now, where're the forks and knives," he mumbled. Once again he glanced up at Cleopas, who urged him on. "Picnic style," he muttered, attempting to scoop up a piece of meat with the unleavened bread.

"You Romans and your metal utensils. You must always stab at something. Wait..." Cleopas's voice rose in sudden blitheness. "You have said it, not I...*ignorant*." He chuckled softly as he made his way to the back room, moments later to return with his hand outstretched. "Here you are. A two-pronged silver device I offer to Romans passing through. To your health, as the Latins say. Now, where were we?"

"My ignorance. About people and things in Palestine," Sam mumbled through a grateful mouthful of food. "Either this is good or I am very hungry and don't give a... Uh, I mean I don't mind at all."

"Yes, that word, *ignorance*. It must not be considered for slander alone. If one does not know the state of affairs then he should become informed. While you eat and while we wait for the *Friend* to appear with the answer to the offer I made Pilate, I shall take the blight of ignorance from your soul called Roman."

Friend! The man in the hospital... Sam wondered at Cleopas' usage. He smiled. "I'm all ears," Sam finally replied politely as he broke bread before the fire. He watched his host pace the floor, the hearth's glow casting a giant-like shadow of the man against the far wall, a shadow that now danced theatrically, one not so beaten and down as it had been when this Cleopas first greeted him an hour before.

"Very well, then," Cleopas began. "As you know, we have a Roman governor appointed by Tiberius Caesar himself by the name Pontius Pilate, also known as Procurator. He is a stern man, swift to anger but slow to rule directly over the Jews." He bent towards Sam as if sharing a secret he wanted no one to overhear. "I have made him an offer," he whispered. "Yesterday. To spare the life of the Master. I have saved regularly for the day in which I should reclaim my dignity. The *Friend* brings the answer. Surely Pilate would not execute a man when such a ransom is offered?" Cleopas stepped back and, with a look of concern, held his arms out and hunched his shoulders. Clearly he was hoping Sam, this Roman stranger, would see the logic of his offering. *Would he?* he seemed to be asking.

Sam replied with a shrug, a gaze of non-commitment.

"Well, then," Cleopas started again. "This Pilate, he prefers to keep the peace by turning over all matters of Jewish legal concern to the consideration of another heretic who, ironically, calls himself King of the Jews. Yet, as you know, the man is not even of Jewish birth.

"He is one called Herod Antipas. Herod, after his father of vaunted pride and arrogance called Herod the Great, a murderous madman who reigned for more than 30 years with blood and terror. This same father Herod murdered his own wife and two sons born of her, solely because he had heard a rumor of a plot! A rumor, mind you! Of him Caesar Augustus said it was better to be a pig in the house of Herod than a son. So was the character of the first Herod. But then, surely, you know of this history," Cleopas concluded confidently as he strode back across the hardwood floor of the inn.

"Of course. Herod the Great and his son the current King, Antipas. Well known in Rome," Sam answered.

"This father of the one called Antipas, who in spite of his iniquities, rebuilt Solomon's temple at the sacred place in Jerusalem, the first temple having been destroyed by the Babylonians in Jeremiah's day six hundred years ago. Do I bore you with this history, Samuel?"

Sam wagged his head. "Fascinating," he answered, glancing around the table for napkins, his fingers raised from his bowl of food.

"Forgive me. Here is a bowl of water for your hands," Cleopas apologized. He reached under the table to retrieve a washing dish. "My daughter did not intentionally..."

"No need. Please. I understand. You were saying."

Cleopas easily slipped back into his account. "This Herod, the elder, was murderous, but as equally villainous is his present-day adulterous namesake, that Herod who sits now on the puppet throne. This Herod Antipas, a glorified tax collector for Rome, shares a kingdom with his brother Phillip, a Tetrarch of Perea, whose wife he stole and took for his own.

"Between these two villains, a false state of Israel, a nation that merely imitates the ancient one under King David, exists at the pleasure of your Caesar Tiberius. And now these two crafty fiends who sit upon thrones made by your Rome, piously call upon our own High Priests to rule in a way they never could, and they know it very well. The real rulers are the Priests.

"Hebrews follow one God, Yahweh. And they follow only a King who should be anointed, as was Saul and David the Bethlehemite of old times, by a prophet of God himself. That prophet bore your very name!" Cleopas delightedly exclaimed as he paced the floor.

"The ancient prophet Samuel anointed, by command of God, Saul and David. Now that is how we should be ruled. God calls, a prophet anoints, and the man rules according to God's desires, not his own. But, alas, there have been no prophets until John called the Baptist, whom Herod caused to be beheaded some two years ago for speaking out against him. So you can see the sorry state of affairs we of Israel are in with no legitimate ruler or king."

Sam gave a slight nod of the head. "Kings come and go, Cleopas. The Caesars themselves manipulate their 'godhood' status. Everyone in Rome knows that. As for your prophets...it sounds like a nice system, but impractical. Power and the lust of it is the only driving force that has ever sustained politicians, kings and their thrones."

"I fear that you are at least correct in the latter case," Cleopas granted. "But men must trust God. And He has used the prophets very effectively through the centuries. Alas, it is us, the children of God, who give no heed to their words. The system, as you call it, nor the prophets, must not be blamed. We fail God's plan for us, not the other way around."

"As you say," Sam allowed, beckoning Cleopas to continue.

"Now the High Priests. They are politicians of another ilk. Many, though not all, use God to cover their sins and pride. To make matters worse, they govern the people upon a foundation of more than six hundred laws set up under Moses's rule, laws put in place to guide the people toward obedience until they finally reached the light of God itself. Once you can see the light of God for yourself, the rules, laws, all of it, are unnecessary. The light teaches you how to live, behave, and one so blessed desires only to do it. Of course, I would be stoned by the Pharisees for saying so."

"I see," Sam nodded, pulling at the flat bread and dipping the smallest morsel in the bowl.

"Israel at the time was a rebellious people, slaves who had been in exile in Egypt for so many hundred years that they had forgotten their God," the innkeeper went on. "They literally had to be taken by the hand and led out of captivity by the prophet Moses. The Mosaic law guaranteed that the people would obey. It took their very hand – and feet too – guiding them in a straight and narrow path. It gave them discipline, that which they lacked. The law held them to a path with the purpose of leading them to see their full potential and, in time, to gain a spiritual-based obedience so that they would recognize their Messiah when He appeared.

"Now the High Priest Caiaphas, along with his father-in-law Annas, himself a former high priest, have created a power base in Judea upon which Herod depends for peace to exist in the land. As long as there is peace, Rome is happy and Herod's position is secure. Do you follow me on this, Samuel?"

"Indeed," Sam answered, thinking back on all the politicians he had interviewed over the past thirty-five years. "Yes, I do follow you. Things don't change much, do they?" he murmured, draining the last droplet of wine from his flask.

"I am afraid they do not. If I didn't believe what the Master had said about his very imminent return in glory, I fear one thousand, two thousand years from now, we may not see much improvement – so stubborn and self-serving is mankind. But then the world could never last that long with the wickedness, warfare, and corruption that abounds. It would self-destruct long before then," Cleopas mused aloud.

Sam spewed the last trickle of wine he was swallowing, then coughed and choked as if something had lodged in his wind pipe. Cleopas hurried to him. Patting his back somewhat vigorously, he asked, "The wine is too strong? Perhaps I have not paid close enough attention..."

"Just thinking," gasped Sam when he'd caught his breath. "I'm fine." He waved his hand, a signal of reassurance. "Go ahead...please."

"More wine." Cleopas again hurried to the back room, leaving Sam to ponder on all that had transpired since he was rushed to the hospital what seemed just hours ago. "Here. Drink," Cleopas insisted.

"En vino veritas," Sam mumbled in reply, taking in a sweet sip of wine.

11

ANNO DOMINI

Could this really be happening? A crack in the wall of time had allowed him to simply wander from his own modern, 21st Century reality back 2,000 years? *Anno Domini!* He thought. *Year of our Lord?*

Dreams. The stuff of the imagination liberally mixed with his final conscious thoughts before drifting off into surgical land - that, mixed with a bit of holiday-season imbibing, in turn mixed with the nagging feeling that his beloved Rachel was, after all, worth any trip he took. A guest on one of his shows a year or two earlier had come with a panel of experts aimed at dissecting his audience's dreams. *"Dreams are the hidden things of the subconscious mind,"* he'd said. *"Symbols, drama, our deepest yearnings are the stuff of dreams."*

"Samuel? Samuel," His host's voice disrupted the gaggle of thoughts swirling about his mind. "I'm sorry for disturbing your reverie. You were many lands away from this place, yes?"

"Oh...yes. Indeed, Cleopas."

"Here you are. More drink. Please." He poured. Sam eagerly drank. "Forgive my rudeness. Perhaps *en vino veritas*, as you say, 'in wine the truth.' I have had so much on my mind this day and night. And you—as if sent from God in this my hour—have come to my house, spy or not, and allowed me to talk, to forget my woes. I have failed you, I fear."

"No, you certainly have not. I admire your hospitality. The wine is very good, by the way. Very good," he repeated.

"More?"

"Yes, please. There is little or no fermentation?"

"I never allow that. It yields nothing but mischief, evil, and foolish behavior from my guests. This is freshly pressed, new wine, stored in earthen jars for your refreshment."

"Thank you," Sam smiled, raising his free hand, signaling for Cleopas to stop pouring. "I don't believe I've ever tasted wine quite like this."

"Then you have never heard my Master's voice," Cleopas sighed, as he began to nervously pace once more. "As I was saying about the many laws of Moses," he continued, "there are laws for washing pots and cups, laws for how many steps one may take on the Sabbath, and laws piled on top of laws, until Moses' original ten have now stretched to over six hundred. The people must obey, or they cannot please God. Their minds," he said tapping on his own covered head, "are so blinded by every Pharisaical prerequisite of worship that they never look up to the sky. If the Messiah came in the clouds, how would they know it? In truth, I tire of it all." Cleopas brought his fingers down over his heart, still tapping lightly. "It is here," he said, "where the law must reside, and that law is love. It is the heart, Sam. It is the heart that gives life to laws, and love to life."

Sam gave a nod. "Profound. Profound indeed. We have a Latin saying in Rome, *'amor omnia vincit.' Love conquers all.* Now I have heard a master tell me why that is so," he said by way of a compliment.

"You must never call me that."

"What?"

"Master. There is but one Master and one True Shepherd. And I have failed him— " his voice broke. The palm of his right hand now came down hard on his sternum with a sharp crack. "From the first time I turned Him away as a babe until today," he sobbed, "I - I have failed Him."

"You are a man who is very hard on himself."

"I have denied my God."

"But how?" Sam implored. "You do not appear to me to be so foolish."

"I certainly do not believe as the rulers, but..." He shook his head, ashamed. "There was no room - no room at the inn? I told my Master's mother and her husband, Joseph, that I had no room for them that night, that night of nights just over thirty-three years ago. Ha! I sold the prospect of housing the Son of the Highest for two silver coins. Two! Oh, Samuel, you cannot understand what a fool that makes me! I have lived a lie my entire life."

"At this inn?" Sam asked in surprise. "What lie?"

"No. I was the owner of a small but orderly inn many years ago. In another town. It failed miserably. Then it burned to the ground in suspicious circumstance during the great slaughter of the children. Bethlehem... Awful... Shameful... I came here after that. I deserved it all, but the children...their sweet innocence taken so cruelly!"

Sam felt in awe of this first-hand witness. It was but a story, *just a Bible story*, he had reasoned. No one would really kill all the children of a town or village. Then it hit him: *Hitler, gas chambers of World War Two*, he readily reminded himself.

"I am sure even you are aware that Herod – the one called 'the Great,' father to our present ruler – was a vile and wicked man," Cleopas continued, breaking Sam's trance. "He fretted much over the tales of several men of wisdom who had traveled from eastern lands. Indeed, they stopped by my very inn soon after the Holy child's birth. These wise magi, as some termed them, inquired as to the sacred birth of Jesus, for they had seen a proscribed sign in the heavens, long foretold as the sign marking the birth of the Messiah of Israel. They brought treasures—gifts to give to him.

"Herod's scribes unearthed the prophecies that told of a child to be born ruler of Israel, in the City of David, the city named after our beloved and first true king of Israel. The prophecy clearly stated that Bethlehem would be the site of his taking a mortal body; thus, the Messiah child came into the world.

"The wise men called the babe 'King of Israel' to Herod's face. When Herod could not stand the torture, his ego burdened with the thought of another replacing him, he ordered the children of Bethlehem, all those under two years of age, murdered by the sword! And, indeed, after the departure of the three, once they had laid their gifts at the babe's feet and took their leave, came the slaughter."

Cleopas clasped his head in his hands, his palms pressing against his ears. "I still hear the cries of the mothers. See the bloody swords! You cannot imagine! The horror, the wailing... for days and days it continued! You cannot! I was almost relieved when my inn burned to the ground. My beloved Mary and I barely escaped with our lives!"

Sam had sat still as stone through the entire tale, allowing the hush of reverence for the nativity story-telling to go unbroken. He easily recalled the account, the narrative repeated annually across the Christian world. *So this was the one who turned Joseph and Mary away.*

He supposed that if he were concocting this dream it would at least need this dramatic element—the tortured groans of a nameless innkeeper, a man so reviled by Christians for centuries. He waited quietly to hear what Cleopas would reveal next.

"Only this," he pointed above the door, "survived the flames, as if by miracle of God!" Sam gazed up at the carefully honed, Lebanese fir-wood plaque above the door, leather cords leading from it to a peg driven into the wall above.

The words inscribed by a carpenter's chisel had survived intact, though they still bore scorch marks from the fire. "Joseph the carpenter from Nazareth had made it a gift for my uncle Simeon when he came to visit Bethlehem as a lad. I have often wondered..." His voice trailed off.

"Wondered what?" Sam asked eagerly, hoping Cleopas's reenactment hadn't come to a premature end.

"I have wondered... *If* I had let Mary and Joseph take my room that night... *If* I had slept in the stable. What if? Would the inn have burned? Would the touch of the newborn Master have saved it?"

"What do the words say?" Sam asked, intrigued.

"Words?" Cleopas responded in thoughtful but distant tone.

"The words inscribed on the plaque."

"Oh, those words. Yes," he whispered. "This gift, the plaque here above the door, is a greeting to those coming and going. Words from the nameless 'Preacher,' as he is known to us. From the Koheleth, the Hebrew reads:

Go thy way, eat and drink with joy and drink thy wine with a merry heart, for God now accepteth thy works. Live joyfully with the wife whom thou lovest...
for that is thy portion in this life.

"Cleopas?" Sam ventured.

"Yes," the sullen man answered.

"Those are beautiful words. May I copy them in my own native tongue? I do not have pen...paper..." he said, voice trailing off. "A what-do-you-call-it? – a writing instrument and, and, uh... parchment. That's it. Do you have something for me to jot them down with?"

Cleopas returned a blank expression. "Jot them down? You have a strange manner of speaking. You wish to have these words?"

"Yes. Yes, I do. I do not read Hebrew and I would appreciate very much putting those words in my language, above my door someday. I miss my wife, and..."

"Then it is yours. You may take this," Cleopas said as he reached above the entry door, intent to remove the sign.

"Oh, no! Cleopas - I would have to earn something so precious. I couldn't. I..."

"I insist."

Sam held up his hand to stop him.

"You truly wish to earn this, then?"

"Yes."

"You are a stubborn man, Samuel Antonius. I have one thing more precious to me than these words and what it represents."

"What is that?" Sam asked.

"My good name!" he cried. "I will be forever known as the first mortal to reject the King of Israel. Can you imagine how that makes me feel? How may I redeem myself?" Cleopas let out a muffled moan. Sam shuddered upon hearing it. Though soft and brief, it issued from deep within, from a sadness that reached to the man's very core.

"I must find a way to report the truth to the world," came the simple reply. "I imagine going back in time and being wiser. I pray for someone to..." He stopped. Turning slowly, he fixed his gaze on Sam, deep in thought. Then a smile creased his lips as a sudden revelation opened itself to him. His expression shifted from dour to vibrant. "Yes! You could do that for me! You are powerful!"

"Do what, Cleopas?"

"You, a man who knows the libraries where the words are made and kept, and you, from the most powerful nation on this earth!"

Sam nodded in agreement but remained silent.

Cleopas paced with nervous energy as if a grand discovery of enormous consequence had just opened to him. "Would you consider it, Samuel Antonius? I shall give this most rare and precious object to you, with one request. You may indeed earn the plaque above the entry to this humble inn!"

"How?"

"Make a report. Tell the world I did not betray Him! And I shall deliver to you the single remaining miracle from the day of our Savior's birth in Bethlehem!"

Cleopas strode back across the room and sat across the table from his guest, locking his moist and tired eyes with Sam's. "If the plaque be not enough, then everything I have, all my earthly possessions are yours for this one thing I ask." His head bowed in humble acceptance of the rejection he expected to receive. "You are busy, of course," he muttered almost inaudibly.

Sam's inner ear reverberated with the voice from the now invisible guide from the hospital: *Grant him an interview and also his request. You may yet live.*

"I'll do it," Sam cheerily offered. "This will make a great Sam...uh, Samuel Antonius Report."

Cleopas slowly raised his head, once again fixing his gaze on Sam. "You are not mortal. Samuel, you surely are an answer to my prayers. Angels come disguised... Are you...?" Cleopas stood and again respectfully bowed his head.

Sam chuckled aloud at the very thought. "I assure you," he said, "those who know me would not liken me to an angel. Far from it. I like you, Cleopas. And I will earn that plaque and those words with my report."

The innkeeper's eyes welled up anew. "Oh, Samuel!" he gasped. "You are a friend, indeed. A blessing! May God forever bless you, your house, your posterity!" Cleopas reached across the table and grasped Sam's hands in his to thank him.

"Cleopas?" Sam interrupted while clearing his throat.

"Yes?"

"Are you for real?" Sam expected the question to either burst the bubble of his surgery-induced fantasy, or to convince himself that something beyond the natural realm was in control after all.

"Sadly, I am real," he allowed, lapsing into his former melancholy almost as suddenly as the cloud of despair had been lifted at Sam's acceptance of the offer. "But at times it all seems like a nightmare. If only I had given up the room. I turned them away! Then the killing started. Oh Samuel...I am a condemned man!" he cried out, pacing, wringing his hands, his eyes now and again flitting toward the door in desperation. "But you will help clear my name. At least I have that hope! Where is he?"

"Who?"

"The one we call *Friend*." Cleopas stopped near a window and peered through a half-closed shutter, hoping to see the Roman band approaching.

The 'friend,' Sam wondered. Once again he had heard the title man at the hospital referred to himself as...

"Where is my *Friend*?" fretted the innkeeper. "What is keeping him?" He moved to the door. Cracking it open, he gazed up the dusty road leading toward Jerusalem.

"Cleopas," Sam interjected. "You said babies were killed. I had thought it a fabrication, surely a legend. I had heard of it, but I could not believe...no man would...it doesn't seem reasonable..." Sam stuttered. "I thought it was a Bible story..."

Cleopas stopped pacing and turned to face Sam. Sternly and with emphasis placed on each word, he intoned, "I assure you it was not! As for *bible*, I know of no such place or thing."

"Stories from a book...a compendium of books, really, A..." Sam paused, stumped at how to explain it all. He pictured himself the playwright of his own production. Yet this player, this actor before him, he seemed so tangible, so heart-broken, so...*real*. This nocturnal illusion of mind and imaginings was no doubt the realization of a lifetime of doubts ebbing to the surface. It was the holiday season, after all. *And after what I told Cardinal McIntyre about needing to see in order to believe, about interviewing everyone but God himself...*

"Samuel?"

He heard his name called. But it was distant.

"Samuel," it demanded.

It was a voice coming from somewhere beyond these walls, felt as much as heard.

"Are you awake, Samuel?"

Rachel often called him *Samuel* when she was worried or angry.

"Focus," he demanded of himself. "Sam. Wake up. Sam..."

Like a vortex eliminating the native gravitation of reality—or life as Sam knew it to be—this psychological drama had replaced the familiar by swallowing the surroundings of home, real people, the hospital. He heard the voice more clearly. Cleopas, his imaginary friend from the time of Anno Domini, had suddenly vanished.

"Samuel? Sam... Come on now, honey. Are you in there?"

12

50/50

"Doctor Peterson, why won't Sam wake up? Did the surgery go well? It's been 24 hours. Surely the anesthetics would have worn off. What if he...?

"Rachel," the doctor broke in. "Something like this can be very traumatic. I don't mean to alarm you, but let's look on the bright side. He's alive. There was, after all, a 50/50 chance..."

"Sam, honey," she called out as she leaned over him. "Samuel, come on," she pled. "I know you can hear me."

He lay, comatose, in the critical care unit, a private room. His only answer to her was a machine-monitored vital sign indicating his newly rebuilt heart was pumping—albeit weakly—on its own, but breathing was still aided. Tubes ran from every opening in his body, both to feed him and eliminate poisons and waste.

"He's so white, so pale, so...deathly. Is that normal?" Rachel asked, the hint of control in her voice quickly giving way to a deep sobbing. "I - I love him. It can't be..."

I love you too, baby, he thought back. Unable to open his eyes, her voice so far away and faint, yet Sam knew she was with him. He struggled to say or do something, anything, to let her know.

Doctor Peterson observed Sam's responses, shining a light into his eyes and tapping his chest, only to find his sensory perceptions seemingly at a standstill.

"Can he come out of it? Doctor, please?" she cried.

I'm here Rachel! I'm in here! Don't give up on me! I'm alive! Dreaming of you, baby! he tried to say through paralyzed lips, eyes shut tight with the heaviness of a fatigue that dominated any power of self-determined control.

"Rachel, it's simply too soon," Doctor Peterson said. "This can go either way. I want you to get some rest. Let's give the staff time to do what they have to and allow Sam to rest. The surgical team has done all they can. Time for love and prayers, Rachel. Come, now."

"Samuel, honey. Don't give up," she cooed, whispering into his ear. "I love you, Sam." She kissed him, letting her tears tumble from her cheek to stain the pasty skin above his brow. "Sleep, darling, but wake a new man; *be whole*...for me."

13

DRAMA UNFOLDS

"Samuel? Samuel? Are you awake?" the deep voice probed.

Sam looked up from the table. He clutched the heavy goblet of wine in trembling hands. He squinted through the mental fog at his benefactor, offering no reply, just groggily peering through the heavy-lidded eyes of a man who had weathered a long, traumatic mental journey.

"Samuel Antonius. Be awake. We have another guest arriving soon. I have bored you...as it appears, nearly to death. And now I fear you will think of me, as others have. That I, an innkeeper born to my trade to house the King of heaven and earth, and a man given to tirades concerning my nation's ills, is in a word, delusional."

"Delusional? No," muttered Sam. "I might be, but not you."

"I did not hear you, my friend," Cleopas answered.

"I am your friend?"

"Yes. Why, yes. I feel you must be, to listen so patiently."

Sam shrugged his achy shoulders. "I interview people. I'm used to it."

"Sullen. So somber. Have my stories of sadness so filled you that you are overcome?"

"I miss her..."

"Ah... The woman! I understand now. A day without my Mary is like a day without air, without food. I hunger for her presence even now. But soon we will be on our way to Jerusalem – as soon as the Roman *friend* arrives, that is. I will see my beloved there. She waits with the others. But you! You must wait to see your woman. I am sad for you, Samuel."

"I will see this through. I only hope I can see her again. It's so strange, this dream. You. It seems so real, yet so very, very foreign. Do you understand? You are an apparition, not real, Cleopas. This is all make-believe."

"The wine. Perhaps it has..."

"No, the surgery! My heart! I have heart valve damage! Coronary artery disease! I am asleep and you keep waking me up! Rachel... She needs me."

Cleopas stood facing him, his mouth agape but silent. A look of compassion swept over him. He had learned much about the musings of lonesome guests. Far-flung travelers often became forlorn and embittered. He had heard many stories...ramblings from men far from home, isolated from loved ones, cut off from familiar surroundings.

This one, though, he was different. Out of place here—dreamy, not in touch with present-day realities. In fact, Cleopas had wondered if it were he, not this man, who was caught up in a dream. The nightmare of the past two days had caused him now to awaken in a numb, petrified melancholy, even weighed down to a near death-like feeling of despair. At least this man represented a form of divergence from the gloom, a willing audience for his pent-up hopelessness. Samuel had roused within him a momentary happiness on this day of sad expectations.

"How are the rulers, then?" Sam croaked through sluggish voice. "You were speaking earlier of the rulers." He swirled the wine in his goblet, studying the dark purple eddy created by its tiny orbit, fully aware that he may already be dead, that this was the place to which he'd been consigned for having ever doubted.

Cleopas sighed, and reached for the flask of wine. "May I share?"

"Certainly," Sam said, pouring liberally.

Cleopas took a healthy gulp, wiped at his mouth with his sleeve, and recommenced his nervous pacing. "The beneficiaries of the Jewish people's observance of the laws are the sect of lawyers..."

"Hah! You have lawyers here too?" Sam bellowed, disrupting Cleopas' monologue. Then he straightened his back and bowed his head, realizing the *faux pas* he had just committed.

Cleopas frowned and shook his head. "Yes, and as I was leading to, lawyers make up the main body of priests of the Sadducee party, and some of the Pharisees who collaborate as well. It is a strange state of affairs. It is a two-party system. Now how can that be effective?"

"I can't imagine," Sam chuckled, shaking his head in acknowledgment.

"I will tell you how. They compromise. They give each to the other to help themselves stay in power and, in so doing, burden and crush the life out of the people. Compromising principle..."

"Exactly!" Sam exclaimed, unable to contain himself. "I was trying to make that very point the other night with Newt Gingrich and Bill Clinton!" He looked at Cleopas, who stood there totally dumbfounded by what Sam was saying. "Please, go on," Sam motioned with a smile.

"You cause me delight, Samuel, though I don't know why. Some for the things you say – and, for that matter, things you don't say. But you are Roman. I must train you." He let out an audible sigh. Then, to Sam's amusement, he lashed out again with the seriousness of a country preacher on the serpentine nature of lawyers.

"The priestly rulers conspire with Herod Antipas, whom they despise, and Antipas in turn conspires with Procurator Pilate, whom he also despises, and Pilate appeases them all to keep Tiberius happy in Rome – whom it is said, he, Pilate, despises.

"Now, the Priests grow fat on the tithes and offerings and sacrifices of the people - it is they who control the money changers at the Temple - and it is they who Jesus of Nazareth condemned more strongly than even Herod or Caesar."

"A question of you, Cleopas," Sam interjected. He felt himself slip into his role of reporter. This monologue was entertaining and enlightening, but it lacked objectivity. "Why condemn the rulers for the state of affairs? Why not blame – and forgive me, but I am gentile – the God of the Jews? After all, if, as all your prophets have taught, Israel is the chosen people, you'd think He would give them a break from all this madness, persecution, burdens and *unholy* state of affairs." Sam nodded, confident that he'd made his point. "Further, if this is what you call being *chosen*, I believe I must retain my gentile sympathies." There. Now he had lit the fire. Now he would get some real answers.

Cleopas launched into a succession of long paces across the creaky, hardwood floor. Sam could sense the anger building. But then, inexplicably, it quickly subsided. The innkeeper sat back down and poured himself a glass of wine. He would turn the tables on this Roman. Without doubt, he would enjoy the theatrics sure to follow.

"You are a proud Roman, but mean no harm," Cleopas finally tendered, together with the release of a deeply held lungful of air. Then he pointed at Sam and accused, "You do not know of what you speak." With that, he began stroking his beard nervously, obviously seething with anger but then alternating with compassion for his guest's lack of understanding. "I struggle to respond to your ignorance. I do not say it to offend you. In former days I would accuse you in my heart of blasphemy, and heatedly vilify you, but now – "

"Now?" Sam asked.

"Are you truly unacquainted with the events of these past days?"

"In Jerusalem?"

"You truly are without knowledge? This is not some trick designed by Herod, Caiapas, or Pilate, perhaps, to try to trap me or the other disciples?" Cleopas wanted to trust Sam. The man's offer to tell his story, help him regain his name, seemed so sincere.

Sam met the innkeeper's stare, poker-faced, waiting, and giving Cleopas the speaker's gavel. There was no need for him to interrupt the man now.

"I, Cleopas, admit my ignorance," the innkeeper continued in meek tones. "But you – you mustn't play me the fool!" he spat.

Sam nodded submissively. "I am a wealthy man where I come from," he replied. "I have spent my time in work and the pursuit of pleasure. I have never prayed to a God, because I can buy my problems away with money.

"But now, for the first time in my life I have questioned immortality. Now there is one I love, and I..." Sam's voice trailed off. "And I need to know if I will ever see her again," the words spilled out, almost reverently. "I don't know if there is a God, or who your God really is. I do not pretend to be a candidate for conversion, but I have a long history of interviewing people with hard questions; so that I might learn the truth..."

Cleopas had stopped his pacing. He now gazed into Sam's eyes, long and hard. "I can read a man's face. You are sincere...but, still *ignorant*."

"Ignorance is no vice, Cleopas," Sam answered. "Perhaps uninformed would be more polite."

"Perhaps. I will cease to condemn you then, or seek to find any other purpose for your visit to me. And, I suppose you must inquire. I will boldly and truthfully answer all your questions. I will never run again!" As to underscore his steadfastness, he struck the open palm of one hand with his fist. "I will begin by telling you of a day of days and a night of nights. It was two nights ago, and..."

14

BE WHOLE!

"I cowered. I, like the other eleven, fled before the Roman guards who escorted the traitor Judas Iscariot past the Temple to the grove of trees the night before last; the eve of Passover.

"I had been gone just a short time from this inn, compelled to journey to Jerusalem to be with and support the Master's followers. I was bringing victuals to the brethren who waited with Him while he prayed. Oh, they had eaten the Passover meal with the Master, but I was not invited. And why should I have been? After all, it was I who turned him away the very first time. I never expected Him to even glance my way..." he said, drifting off into silent reverie.

Sam waited. "You were bringing victuals..."

"I beg your forgiveness," mumbled Cleopas. "I, ah, yes. I was bringing more food for when they should return to the upper room, the room above the home of the young man and his mother. One named John Mark."

"You were at *The Last Supper?*" Sam blurted.

"I...the last supper?" Cleopas frowned.

"Forgive the interruption. Please continue..."

"As I was saying, I thought if I comforted the Apostles with nourishment - figs, dates, bread - they might endure the day to come - the Sabbath, you know. Mark, the same young man from Jerusalem in whose house the disciples had often met, was with me. A brave lad! A very brave lad, indeed!" he sighed bringing his hands to his head, searching the strands of memory woven the night before last, feeling the sudden pain and anguish as if a throbbing pain had overtaken him.

"But it was just an innkeeper's mentality, to feed the gathering, to try to make up in any way for missing the hospitality I might have shown the infant child of Joseph and Mary. And I felt a keen desire to be near my Master, for I somehow knew - though did not want to believe - that he was foretelling a fate to come to him, a certain doom that caused us to despair."

Sam sat respectfully quiet. Ruminations of the Bible story coming to him now, this man was filling in the gaps to a story that had been told and retold countless times over the past two millennia.

"As I was saying..." Suddenly Cleopas embarked on a recounting of his Passover eve exploits with John Mark —

***

"You must be very quiet, John Mark," the older man motioned, his finger to his lips. "This is a Passover like no other," he assured the young follower of the Galilean.

Both men peered across the courtyard to the open window, where the gathered disciples were listening to the Master as he broke bread for the Seder.

"He looks so solemn, Cleopas," the young man whispered. "I wish I were in there with them," he sighed. "Why do you suppose we were not invited? He knows we are here. He has never denied us before."

"There is something wrong," Cleopas cried under his breath. "I feel it. I feel it as if a lion is about to spring from the darkness and attack without warning."

"There! Who is that leaving by the back steps?"

"Judas; probably on an errand for the Seder."

"Judas? The one who keeps the purse for the disciples...on an errand? He appears in a hurry."

"Indeed."

The two men remained in the shadows, just feet away from where the disciples, now minus one, were attending the Passover with their Galilean leader. "Cleopas, why have you not stayed at your inn this night?" asked Mark. "It must be crowded with pilgrims come to celebrate the Holy Days here in Jerusalem. Are you not afraid that someone might take advantage of you while you are away?"

"Not when you have as a friend a Roman Centurion who has billeted his men for the period of the feasts. Within an easy march of the city gates, all my guests know to return each evening to guard against road thieves and villains."

"Is he in truth a *friend*?"

"He is. Those of us who know him, know him to be a follower of our Lord. He cannot reveal his name to any save a few. Therefore, we know and call to him simply as *the Friend*. It would not go well with him among his Roman superiors to reveal his sympathies. But he does much for our cause and is a righteous and a just man according to all the laws of the Jews."

"What is the Master doing now?" queried John Mark. "His manner of breaking the bread, holding it up for everyone to see...he does not dip it where he did the bitter herbs..."

"I do not know. He is speaking. John Mark, go to the door. Hurry. Tell me what you hear him saying."

Mark hurried out of the room and mounted the steps beneath the open window, crouching in the shadows.

"Take, eat..." he heard; words soft but clear from Jesus. Holding aloft the pieces of broken bread, Jesus invited each to partake. "This is my body and a new covenant..."

***

"And thus ended the supper," sighed Cleopas, finishing the account of what Mark had both seen and heard that night. "That is what took place in that upper room, perhaps our Lord's final Passover in this life." Then he slumped onto the bench next to the rough hardwood serving table and buried his head in his arms, released a heavy groan, took in a deep breath and held it inside. Sam watched; saying nothing.

"I was a coward," he muttered, unleashing the self-loathing from his lungs. "I have wept many tears this day for my cowardice. At least Simon stood against them. And John Mark! You should have seen him come up to be near, just behind an olive arbor - there, ready to stand by Peter! A boy, but such a man! But I remained there in the shadows, where - with mine own eyes - I saw the whole affair."

Sam stopped him. "You saw the agony of your Master in the Garden of Gethsemane?"

"Garden? I never thought of the orchard a garden. But, yes, I did see my Master kneel on the ground..."

Silence—

"You are a firsthand witness to this?" Sam asked again, taken aback by the revelation.

"You say you have not yet been to Jerusalem—that you come from Rome directly? Yet you know the name of the grove so named for the olive press? How?"

"Books. Maps."

"Ah yes.... your 'books,'" Cleopas said knowingly. "Well then....You will report this account to others, no doubt?" Cleopas asked.

"I may. Yes, I may...with your permission."

"Permission? I have no fears! Not any more! I will let the entire world know that the once cowardly innkeeper was a witness to the miracle birth, and arrest of the Messiah, Jesus of Nazareth. But I fear I may never be given the opportunity to clear my name, be that witness. I fear generations will simply revile me; my poor name."

Sam knew that Cleopas's fears were not unfounded. Insofar as the Bible account was concerned, people for two thousand years would remember the greedy innkeeper of Bethlehem and, indeed, vilify him for his avarice and cowardly lack of concern for the laboring mother of the Son of God. The reporter laid a hand on the innkeeper's arm. "That is why records are so very valuable. You must write it down. I will share it with the world if you do," he promised.

"You make me a pledge? A vow?" Cleopas spoke reverently now, with hopeful voice; wide pleading eyes.

"If I ever get home again, I promise to share your story, and exactly as you recount it."

"Then you must hear the rest of the tale!"

Sam nodded for him to continue.

"I followed the disciples from a discreet distant and buried myself in the shadows of the grove of trees," Cleopas went on, at once lost in the memories of a few nights earlier. "The disciples were weary. They lay on the ground near the gate and slept. Jesus walked on several dozen paces from there, and knelt down beside a large stone at the base of an ancient olive tree, one in the grove correctly called Gethsemane.

"It was not long after that I witnessed Judas Iscariot, one of the Apostles, approaching. But before he reached us, Jesus, garments caked to his body as if he had perspired in blood, then staggered from the shadows and gently rebuked his disciples: '*Canst thou not wait with me this one hour?*' I almost gasped aloud when I saw Him. At first I thought someone must have attacked him while he prayed. Still, there he stood in the full moonlight, proud, tall, manly, in a majesty only he could display, a manner familiar to those of us who had seen him teach. Then Judas, that traitor of the twelve, kissed him on the cheek, correctly saying '*Master,*' after which Jesus said, '*Betrayest thou the Son of man with a kiss?*'"

Cleopas paused to draw a breath, his tender, raw emotions evident in his far-off stare. "Then the guards, with drawn sword, came forward – but not before Simon interceded. He withdrew a scabbard from his belt and struck at the man nearest, the High Priest's chief servant, Malcus. Malcus just stood there, stunned, then screamed in pain as he realized his right ear had been severed from his head by Simon's sword.

"And what I witnessed next – this would make a believer of anyone, I tell you. Simon threatened the guards and berated Judas as he positioned himself between them and the Master.

"But he, Jesus, came forward and bent to the ground to retrieve what I suppose was the ear of Malcus. When he brushed past Simon, the guards recoiled in fear, as if the Master would smite them with something mightier than a sword.

"But the Master merely stretched his hand out to touch the wounded servant and said, '*Be ye whole,*' and it was done! At that, Malcus fell back, caressing the side of his head with his hand. Finding no blood, and the ear restored, he wondered greatly and the crowd marveled aloud, until, that is, another, a Priest from the Sanhedrin, commanded the guards with the words, '*Seize him!*' as if the gentle Master were a threat...

"Why his robes were drenched in blood, I knew not. I have not as yet spoken with Simon. I am greatly wondering now. For when they seized the Master we all fled. I came directly here, and have talked to no one, excepting the Roman messenger, our secret friend who delivered the ransom notice from me to Pilate. You, now, are the only other to whom I have divulged so much history. Strange, both of you Romans and yet I feel perfectly safe. Indeed, strange," Cleopas concluded, yet lost in thought.

"You said something," Sam prodded. "You said he used words to put the servant's ear back on?"

"Yes."

"Say them again for me, please," Sam asked solemnly.

"'*Be ye whole.*' He said the words, 'Be ye whole,' and then I ran. Why?" Cleopas asked rhetorically. "I abandoned him. My wife did not, nor did any of the women abandon him." He shook his head sadly. "Even John surnamed Mark followed the entourage with the bound Master. So fearless! But me... Ah, the greedy man I was the first time he needed me revealed himself again. But then, coming to myself once I safely arrived here at the inn, I quickly realized my error and sent the offer of money with the Centurion."

Sam offered no response. He sat, took in the large brooding man who so easily swung from one overcome by melancholy, to bold defender of the faith, to hospitable host.

"Oh, where is the Roman band, and my friend Centurion Cornelius?" Cleopas exclaimed. The silence of the spacious room echoed no answer.

Sam raised an eyebrow. *Friend? Centurion? Cornelius?* His thoughts shifted again. *Be ye whole*, he thought. Words Rachel said were used in her childhood dream of being made well. *Be ye whole.* Words she used again moments ago at his intensive care bedside as she tried to kiss him awake. He could still hear her plea, 'Sam, *be whole*,' spoken with all the tenderness and faith and certainty of her being – as if it had already happened, just as it had in her healing from death's grip as a child. Likewise, the guide, the white-robed man at the hospital after surgery, used those exact same words...

Looking around him, Sam longed to see her now, wished he had not once again slipped so easily back into this dream, this death, this whatever-it-was. He returned his attention to the innkeeper, determined to find answers to the question, continue to play the investigator in this mental mystery – his reason for this soul-travel to a place and time he'd deemed no more than the fanciful fairytales and notions of the hopeful, those resting their faith in a God.

"You said Cornelius?" Sam offered in the ponderous quiet of the dining hall.

"Shhh," the big Hebrew motioned to his lips as guests started filing in from their devotions in Jerusalem. "It is dusk. The Sabbath ends and the guests return from the Temple." He signaled towards two men entering the inn and placing their belongings in a corner before taking seats at a nearby table. "Come, follow me," he said to Sam.

Parting a curtain leading to a back room, Cleopas led Sam into a kitchen area. "Daughter," he called out in hushed tones, "the guests arrive. Call for our help to come. Go, child. Quickly!" The young woman who had been preparing food simply nodded and slipped out a back door.

"One cannot be too careful. I must not speak of the Roman Centurion at this dangerous time. But then, I already have," he reasoned to himself. "Well, then, Roman scribe Samuel Antonius, you will meet him soon, and no doubt you yourself may inquire of him. Soon the inn will be filled with strangers, all talking of the events of these days. I must go to the city, to Jerusalem, and, if at all possible, redeem myself of my cowardice."

Sam was a skilled observer of human nature. Cleopas, surely, was one unique individual, a sincere person, one without guile. And this discussion he'd been having was as real as any of the thousands of interviews he'd done over the years. Though still convinced that the hospital anesthesia was working overtime on his mind, wearing off all too slowly, if he actually was dying, Sam reasoned, "Why not go out being entertained?"

"Yes, Cornelius," the innkeeper whispered, pulling Sam from his reverie. "But you mustn't mention his name if you are a true friend to us. I trust you will honor my request, a man from Rome on an investigative journey?" said Cleopas nervously.

"Is his name so secret that it should not be mentioned in connection with the others? With you?" Sam posed, now playing experienced journalistic reporter.

Cleopas frowned, then took to pacing; didn't answer directly. "Romans are hardly tolerated, much less liked. In all the confusion of the Christ, our Messiah, Cornelius was one Roman who shared his conviction with one named Simon Peter. He had seen Jesus do a miracle, heal one of his servants by the mere mention of words. But a more sure witness resides within the Centurion, in here." Cleopas patted the center of his chest. "He has befriended our cause and it must not be made known of his sympathies. Not yet. Not in all the confusion of these days."

"Cornelius is a well-known name in Rome," Sam ventured. "A noble family," he added with uncertainty.

"So they say. But this one is an Iberian, being adopted at birth by one Senator Cornelius after a fearsome battle in which his parents suffered death by the hands of legionnaires."

"So not a true nor pure Italian of Rome?"

"No, Iberian. What do the Roman dogs know of purebred races, anyway? They conquer, vanquish, intermarry. It means nothing."

"I see. And being a Hebrew, of one race, one house, means something?"

"I must confess, you seem so terribly informed of the trials of God's chosen people. How could you even ask that – unless, of course, you mean to insult me?"

"I mean no injury. It seems to me with all this talk about the Son of God, and the chosen people, and a Messiah, that you of this land see him as a Savior to you alone. Was he not a man for all, if he healed the servant of a Centurion; a Roman? Perhaps he was a special soul from God who came to heal more than the wounded pride of the House of Israel?"

"You are treading on ground you know not of, Samuel. But it surprises me, really; your last statement. You have perceived, in all your ignorance of our confused state of affairs, that He, Jesus of Nazareth, was really a Messiah for all. Judeans, Galileans, Samaritans! Imagine that, the despised Samaritans are being baptized and won to his cause!

"It confuses me, but the more I meet people such as the Centurion, I think perhaps His salvation is not of this world. Oh, He talked of another world, but we were eager for him to take the throne to which he rightfully could lay claim.

"I have not understood this clearly, mind you. But I am sensing His mission to be more than we understood. But it is lost now," he said in a low voice. "All lost," he repeated as he paced with head hung, pensive, moodily solemn.

"What if I were to tell you the name of Jesus will go down as one of history's most remarkable and revered men?"

"Ah, how? Who would think of it?"

"Perhaps millions. Perhaps hundreds of millions."

"There are not that many Jews. Even if all of Italia, Iberia, Macedonia, Thracia, Greece, Britannia, all of the known world were to believe his message, I hardly think..."

"Not now, but in future generations. Say you wrote down the stories in a book, and later the book was circulated, and someday the book were to be made available to every household. Then?"

"Impossible to think such things, such nonsense. Book? This new word you continue to use... Scrolls are not kept in such quantities. I admire your creative thought. But as a librarian of the Senate, I suppose you must think in such possibilities. No, my Roman friend. This is the end of a bright flame, a flame of hope that has now been snuffed out before it could begin to burn in the bosoms of the millions you speak of. Like so much chaff is blown to the wind during threshing time, our dreams are scattered too." He strode the floor more vigorously. With the tide of melancholy coursing through him, the powerful man could not stay still. "I have but one request of you, Samuel," Cleopas said, drawing nearer and laying a massive hand on the shoulder of his visitor. "You mustn't mention at any time, nor anywhere, the name of Cornelius when you speak of the disciples. No one must know of his association, his connection with us. Do you take an oath?"

Sam sagged under the arm of the burly Judean, and realized the magnitude of the body that shielded an equally heroic spirit. While he felt no fear, the Jew's intent was sure. *Do not mess with my people.*

"I promise to keep your secret."

"Well done, then," he replied, loosing Sam from his grasp. "What could be keeping our *friend?*"

15

CENTURION

So now he, Cornelius, a pagan, according to Jewish law, and his band of Legionnaires trudged down the dusty road from Jerusalem, with designs of staying the night at the same way station and village of Emmaus that had been their first stop on their route to the coast. Only hours earlier he, along with Tribune Valerius, had take part in an event that had chilled his blood in a way that all the battles he'd ever fought had not.

Valerius is a swaggering dog, not fit for the kennels of a canine. He is the reason Rome suffers ill repute. And a true coward; a first-rate bully. If I were not sworn to my oath as a Legionnaire, I'd...

He suspended such treasonous thoughts as the image of the suffering man on the cross from earlier in the day came back to him. *The man Jesus was no coward*, he told himself.

Cornelius had been a man of the sword for so long that he found it hard to not consider ridding the world of a detestable creature such as Valerius by that means. After all, the mere taking of a life was easily accomplished.

A Tribune! Valerius? Perhaps by rank, but not by honor. Alas, Cornelius had been a Centurion for over a dozen years now, and he would remain one, he supposed, until death. Tribunes were from the upper classes, the privileged ranks of the elite of Rome and her Provinces, and though he a Senator's son as well, it was well known he was not blood line, but adopted. The elites knew little of the men in the ranks who fought and bled for the Empire. It was the Centurion who, with his select hundred men, changed the course of battles and forged the path to victory. But glory? That was reserved for the officer's corps, and Valerius reveled in his closeness to Procurator Pilate.

Such a contrast was the Tribune from the gentle Galilean who had been nailed on the cross that day. Valerius had shown an inordinate viciousness and cruelty toward the hapless criminals who had flanked the so-called King of the Jews. Indeed, it was a spectacle that almost had brought Cornelius to reach for the hilt of his sword. The pitiful, penetrating gaze of the tired, beaten, yet heroic Galilean had made him think better of dispatching Valerius to the underworld.

Cornelius was no stranger to death. Nor had he been but a passive bystander in past executions. No, assuming the courts had justly passed their sentences, he'd done his duty without pause. Though some men had on occasion met their fate innocently by way of the cross or archer's field, those who were condemned by law were no better than any other man.

Not so with this man Jesus. Cleopas the innkeeper would have wanted me to ransom him, he thought. *Cleopas would have wanted to me to defend him, to say there was still hope for the promised Messiah. In truth, I had sent him such word just this morning by messenger. But now... Now, how do I tell him that not only is there no longer hope, but that I was forced to take part in the very execution of his Messiah?*

16

CORNELIUS

Cleopas peered through the curtains. His staff of servers were occupied; his daughter, too. They all had been trained well. He was satisfied that, for now, the inn was in good hands. *But what of Cornelius*, he posed silently.

A knock at the back door. Then two more taps.

Cleopas smiled over at Sam and gave a nod. Sam remained seated at a small table in the dimly lit corner of this room, mainly used for storage.

"You must forgive me, friend Cleopas," the sturdy Roman announced as he entered the back door. "There are things which happened yesterday that caused my delay. My men await us without. They will follow discreetly behind. I assume you have heard the news?"

"I have not been able to sleep for the commotion in my soul these past hours, ever since they took him away. What hear you, sir?"

"Are my words safe?" the Roman queried, motioning towards Sam.

"He is a Roman. I have been educating him on the sorry state of affairs for some hours, awaiting your arrival. I apologize for not having made proper introductions. This is Samuel Antonius."

"Greetings," Sam offered, stepping out from the shadows. "I am Samuel, an observer in this land."

"Sent by the courts of Rome, no doubt?" pressed the Centurion. "I must warn you now, Samuel Antonius, I am in no mood for intrigue." He rested his grip firmly upon his broad sword and fixed Sam with a fierce gaze.

"I understand," Sam nodded. "Look at my hands," he found himself saying. "They are soft, unlike yours. A journal-keeper's hands. There is no need..." he said to the Roman, his eyes flitting to the soldier's sword.

"I may be of Rome, but I have seen treachery. You must forgive me, but I am in no mood for much inquiry. Not now. Not today."

"Come, my friend," bade Cleopas, leading him to a corner dining table, leaving Sam at the far end peering out a small window toward a setting sun. "Your soldiers? They are billeted outside the inn?"

"They are," the sturdy Roman returned. "Half stay and half of the band accompany us up to Jerusalem. What do we have to do with this man?" he asked in an annoyed whisper, pointing to Sam.

Cleopas gave a slight hunch of the shoulders. "I am not sure. He has appeared out of nowhere. I do not know what to make of it. His Aramaic is impeccable, yet he asks to go to Jerusalem as if he has never seen this land. Truly educated, yet he seems naive and unsure of himself. I do not suspect him of foul intentions - not yet. He is either a very good actor on the stage of conspiracy or a complete newcomer to this land, as he claims. His clothes are remarkably well maintained for having journeyed up the road from the port of Caesarea. New robes, unlike I have ever seen. Very strange."

"So they are. I will inquire of him," Cornelius replied, lowering his voice.

"No. Let us play along," Cleopas urged. "Let us find all we can. If it be a ruse, a game he plays, he will surely give himself away. Then we may find his purposes and surely be warned whether this be part of Pilate's scandal or he has been sent from Tiberius Caesar himself."

"Aye. That will be satisfactory. I will play the game with this man. But if he moves to bring one injustice to the brethren, I swear by the heavens, I shall..." He reached again for the hilt of his sword. Daggers equally formed in his eyes as he shot another glance at the visitor.

"Thou shalt not swear an oath, not at all!" Cleopas reprimanded sharply, then kindly added, "The Master required of us a higher thing."

"Samuel Antonius. Your papers, please." The Centurion abruptly stood and challenged the visitor.

Giving no thought, Sam involuntarily reached into his tunic and retrieved them. "Certainly. Here you are," he said, himself surprised at their sudden appearance.

The Roman, tilting the papers toward the candlelight, gave them a cursory inspection. "Hum. Well, then. You are from the Senate - a librarian, it appears. And may I ask your duty here in Palestine?"

"To heal a broken heart," he mumbled. "And to wake up," he added under his breath.

"What? Again man, speak!"

"To inquire. To learn. To report... That is all."

"A spy," Cornelius scoffed.

"I am a reporter – one who sees, hears, and records for history. I have many questions as to why I have been sent here, believe me. I am eager both to learn and to return home." Sam stopped in his tracks. He was surprised at how fluid the words came to his lips, as if rehearsed somewhere before.

"You have family in Rome?"

"I have family, yes, but not in Rome."

"Wife? Children?"

"Yes. Wife and children."

"This is a dangerous land, Samuel Antonius. One so soft as you..." the Centurion mocked, and yet spoke truly, "...traveling alone, one such as you could find himself in grave danger."

"I agree, Centurion. I would ask your intervention. May I travel with you to Jerusalem?" inquired Sam.

"We are going this hour. It is but a few hundred furlongs. As you can see the very lights of the city and temple, even Fortress Antonia and the Governor's Palace come to view with the setting of the sun. Where are you staying this night?"

Sam found himself at an impasse. His mind was here, his body was in recovery now, or...perhaps even dead! He shuddered at the thought. If he could just make all this go away! He turned away from the two men and thought of home, Rachel. He squeezed his eyes shut. *Wake up now*, he commanded himself.

"*Make your report.*" An audible but soft voice whispered into Sam's ear. Startled, he opened his eyes and turned, expecting to see someone there – in truth, to be somewhere else, in recovery, at the hospital, awake.

"I asked you, sir, where do you intend to stay?" the Centurion insisted. He drew closer to Sam, a look of menace in his eyes.

Sam reached out to touch him. *This isn't really happening, is it?*

The barrel-chested soldier countered this perceived threat by sidestepping the blow, seizing Sam's hand and giving it a quick, downward thrust.

Sam recoiled in fright. "Ouch! Hey...you're hurting me! God in heaven!..."

"What say you?" the Roman asked pointedly. "What God speak you of?"

"Just a manner of speech. That hurt!" howled Sam, shaking his hand, then stopping to examining the red mark that was beginning to appear. He believed that dreams held messages, had a certain amount of meaning and purpose. But this was becoming all too painful; painful *and* real.

"Your destination!" Cornelius demanded.

"I am going to Jerusalem. I have been sent to this inn. I have been told one named Cleopas will guide me to where I must make my inquiries. I do not know where I will stay when I reach the city. I seek your advice on the matter," he grumbled, still rubbing his aching knuckles.

"You are playing with me, Samuel Antonius. You may stay at the Procurator's. Any Roman citizen sent from the Senate knows very well he is a guest in the Governor's Palace during this festival of Passover, or any other."

"I am on an unwanted assignment, an unwilling player," Sam returned sharply. He gasped at the next thought that flooded his brain: *I may never wake up, never see Rachel again. What if...this is it! Hell, what I deserve for a life of cynicism, a life without faith... with no belief in God.*

"Very well, then," Cleopas interjected. "Come join us now. We depart for Jerusalem at once. There you will be led by Centurion Cornelius to Pilate's residence, where you may present your papers. Again, I must ask you to promise that there will be no mention of the Centurion's name as to his friendship to the followers of Jesus. Jerusalem is a dangerous place tonight. One could easily be found dead, given the jealousies and suspicions which have invaded our Holy City these past few days."

17

FRIENDS

His journey to another world had seemed more surreal, yet, at the same time, almost natural, as each moment passed. He had heard before of out-of-body experiences. Perhaps this was one. Sam had interviewed mediums and those who professed to have passed on and then returned from beyond mortality. But he had seen no bright lights, no kind judge, no face of God showering love upon him, as was the general story. The Roman soldier had hurt him. He didn't feel love, he was indeed suffering hunger... He felt strangely alive, yet...

His sedation was real – he was sure of that. Rachel had touched him. He was sure of that, too. These drug-induced images were players come to torment him now. *If I'm asleep, if this is in fact just a dream, at least it was proving entertaining as well as enlightening,* he thought as he pondered on his situation. He watched, still massaging the back of his hand.

"Oh, Friend!" squealed Sariah, daughter of the innkeeper, upon seeing the big Roman. She had entered through the curtain separating the dining hall from this back room and immediately flown to him, wrapping her arms tightly around his waist.

"Child," he spoke tenderly as he knelt down near her beaming face. "Such beautiful eyes. I have something for you."

I know that voice, Sam noticed, as the Centurion's declarations softened in tone.

"You mustn't," begged Cleopas, adding, "You are spoiling the girl."

"Let her be spoiled," the Centurion laughed. "It is enough that life is dreary and hard in these times." That said, he dug into a pouch he carried over one shoulder. "For a Princess," he displayed happily, forgetting momentarily the seriousness of life as it was, events as they had turned that day.

"Oh Father! See? A real looking glass! I can see my face! Like holding a pool of waters in my hands," she excitedly exclaimed.

Sam looked on from the dimness of the corner to which he had retreated. *Such humility here,* he thought.

Cornelius's smile widened. "Look, she beams like an angel, dear friend Cleopas. This truly has been worth my trip. The ivory handle is from the coasts of Africa. And the glass from my homeland of Iberia," he boasted, stroking the edge of the mirror.

"I believe she sees an angel in Roman uniform," Cleopas replied. "As do I."

Sam studied the stance of the man, his stature, his athletic build. In appearance, voice and mannerisms alike... *No—that was in my time... Not here; now.*

"Child, is all ready? I know you wish to be merry, but we must be departing shortly," Cleopas said, returning to the more serious matters at hand.

"Father," Sariah chirped, "I have arranged the food stores and have the house in order. What more shall I do?"

Cleopas raised his head, whispered something unheard, and embraced his daughter. "Thank you, child, for your willing obedience. Please go to your cousin at the far end of the village and abide there while I go to Jerusalem. Our hired help shall manage things here. I will return on the morrow."

"You go to see mother? To see John Mark, too?" she asked, her hopeful eyes glinting with moisture.

He smiled down at his auburn-haired child, kissing her on each pale cheek. "Yes. To mother and to your betrothed. I shall send him your loving greetings. Go, now. God be with you, my little lamb."

Sariah dabbed at her eyes with her apron. "And with you, father. I shall pray for you, mother and the others," she offered as she departed. "Shalom, sir," she added, turning in the direction of Sam.

"Yes. Shalom, Sariah," Sam respectfully returned.

She lunged toward the Roman Centurion and wrapped her arms once more around a broad waist burdened with sword and sheath. The looking glass in her hand, she pressed her cheek against his massive upper body.

"God be with you, Sariah," he whispered.

"And with you, *Friend.*"

18

HE IS DEAD

Now that they were on the road, Cornelius tendered the bad news that Cleopas had been too terrified to inquire about. Cleopas had even asked the Centurion to delay the news of his Lord's fate, and the plea and ransom given Pilate to spare the Messiah, until they were on their way. He feared that he might not have the emotional strength to leave the inn for Jerusalem if his worst fears became confirmed.

"Better to be on the journey," he had whispered to the Centurion at the inn. Though now he knew the truth, still he was not taking it easily. He had to stop once to gather himself. Try as he might, he could not accept the fact that he never would be able to redeem himself; that he would never again see his beloved spiritual leader. Cornelius, after delivering the tearful words, had to steady him, and at length, they had resumed the journey.

"I was appointed to carry out the execution," Cornelius finally added. "I initially refused. Then I thought I might find occasion to free him at the last minute, there atop the hill they call Calvary, the place of execution. But...I failed. I lacked the ultimate strength of will to stand against the Empire. Now I wish I had ordered my men against the garrison of the Fortress Antonia. I should have had the courage to set Jesus of Nazareth free. Yet..."

Sam listened intently. The many gaps in the biblical New Testament tale were being filled in before his eyes, even if he was merely concocting this scene in his sleeping subconscious.

"You are no coward, Centurion. I am, but you are not," Cleopas insisted. He hesitated, stopping in the middle of the road. Reaching for his mid-section, he doubled over in agony and fell to the dusty road. "I cannot go on!"

Cleopas wept, unashamed. The Centurion glanced back to his men, some hundred meters to the rear. They would not have seen this demonstration yet.

"Come, Cleopas," he gently urged, hoisting the innkeeper to his feet. "Samuel, assist me, if you please."

Sam hurried forward and took an arm on the opposite side of the soldier. The Centurion again glanced back at his men. "I am fortunate to have such trusted soldiers assigned to my charge," he offered. "I fear, however, that I am out of grace with Pilate," grunted Cornelius as they trudged up the hilly dirt lane headed for Jerusalem's southern gate.

Sam observed and listened as Cornelius explained how his hundred men had been split in two groups to accommodate increased trade along this route. Clearly, his purpose was to ease the mind of Cleopas; divert him with other facts.

"With Quintus, my right hand Sergeant, commanding the fifty in Jerusalem, they were required to do the dirty work of the Governor." So it had been on that day of the execution, Cornelius explained further. "A part of my band are still now stationed in Jerusalem, a part with me here, and others positioned at the port of Caesarea on the coast," Cornelius finished.

Sam watched as these soldiers from the coast hung back to protect the small caravan they accompanied from Emmaus. These had not yet been in Jerusalem this week. Respectful, they were within easy distance to protect their Centurion and his fellows, the innkeeper and himself, and Samuel, the supposed librarian.

"Does he know?" Cleopas questioned, his tone anxious and hurried. He referred to Pilate, the Governor, and his knowledge of the crucifixion of Christ.

Sam fought to keep up. He wasn't used to traipsing further than from the elevator to his studios in the CNTV building on Fifth Avenue. His breathing labored, his muscles ached. The riveting discourse between Cornelius and Cleopas, however, kept him from dwelling on his personal troubles.

"I wasn't able to deliver the ransom note, friend Cleopas," confessed the Centurion. "I was late. But if Pilate does know my allegiance to you and the other disciples, I will lay out a case he shall never forget. I will go against the Empire, if I have to. For that matter, I will go to my father's home and to the Senate, filing a motion to censure Pilate for this murder."

Cleopas wagged his head. "You are more service to us now than ever. What will become of our small Jewish Church?"

"Jewish Church no longer. It is now mine as well; it is all people's. Do not you recall that He commanded your disciples, even Peter, to one day go into all the world?"

"Yes, but there are Jews in all the world," Cleopas kindly rejoined.

"This faith, this belief in goodness, in love, in brotherly service - these healings of the body, spirit and soul are not to be for Jews alone, my dear friend," countered the soldier.

As Sam huffed to keep up, he was stunned at the vision of the one and the lack of insight of the other. *If they only knew how this would grow*, he thought to himself.

"If they, the rulers, find Peter, John, James and the others, will they run?" Cornelius asked candidly.

"No! Never! Not again! Nor will I run! I will offer to be crucified, if I must!" Cleopas swore. "Never will I run again!" He swung his fist as a witness of his determination.

Cornelius was sure of what he would do. Still, he needed to know that he, alone, would not be making a stand; that others would be at his side when the time came. This small assurance brightened him. "Though Jesus be dead, he is buried in the tomb of merchant Joseph of Aramathea, in the garden near where the execution took place. At least we may honor him at our pleasure." Cornelius supposed the fact might lighten Cleopas's heavy mood.

Cleopas lurched to a stop once more. "I know the place. It is true. Oh..." The story of Jesus' death, though described in detail for the last hour by the Centurion, only seemed to sink in deeper with each step he took. All of a sudden, Cleopas felt weak and highly vulnerable. Perhaps it was that he was completely spent from lack of sleep. Or that he had not eaten for two and one half days. Faint, the realization of his Master's demise setting in even more firmly, he stumbled, fell completely to the dusty road as before, and this time let out a frail yet audible sob — the kind of anguished cry a brother might emit at the loss of one he loved so thoroughly.

The sob turned into two, then three. At last Cleopas managed to gasp through his tears, "I can't. I - I can't go there. Let me die here. Tell my Mary... I feel so tired. So completely lost and tired."

Sam watched silently, the journalistic curiosity overtaking him.

"Cleopas! Brother!" the Centurion intoned gently as he shielded his large Jewish friend from the cruel sunlight with his even larger frame. Then Cornelius did something unthinkable, especially in possible sight of his men: he knelt, reached down and lifted the other to his feet, then embraced him, sharing in his friend's private agony. "Come, now," he urged at last. "Time is spent. Jerusalem lies just ahead. We must make haste. You have me to carry you, if I must. You are needed."

"For what?" the overwrought innkeeper whimpered. "He is dead – you yourself witnessed it. It is true?" he asked, as if still in a state of dazed unbelief. "My God, my God, how can this be? I had the money to free him... Why?"

The Centurion did not respond, but stood looking skyward, blinking at the moisture burning his own eyes now. "Yes, I saw. I took the spikes out," his commanding, though soft voice broke. "He is dead, but always with us here." The Centurion rapped the center of his chest.

The caravan and Cornelius's band of soldiers were yet on the opposite side of the hill, had not crested it as these three had. Thus, they had not beheld what had taken place. Even in all his bluster, Cornelius was glad of that. For now, at least, the trust and confidence of his men was vital.

Cleopas at last regained his composure. "I am so weak – oh, may God hear my prayer! Please..." he gritted through the tears.

Sam stood stock still, taking it all in. And for the first time this night of post-surgical repose, he swallowed a bit of salty moisture. He tried keeping his emotions at bay; to maintain the reporter composure he had earned over many years at many celebrated sites of brotherhood in war and peace. But his efforts were in vain. He had been eyewitness to this scene dozens of times, similar manly emotion on the battlefields in Vietnam as a young Army journalist, and more recently for CNTV in the Iraq and Afghanistan wars. Whatever this was – a dream, a visit to the wall of time that melded past history with history's hazy, mystical future, or another dimension he had broken into – he was moved at the depth of feeling here.

"Come, Cleopas. We must go. We could be seen in this awkwardness. I am your brother, indeed, but we must be strong, show strength," implored the Centurion. "Let us deliver Samuel Antonius to Pilate's mansion and be done with him. We shall then repair to seek out the others. Then, I am afraid, I must report to Tribune Valerius."

They plodded onward once more, Sam holding back a few respectful paces but leaning forward to overhear all he could about these two, their doubts, fears, and faith alike. He overheard the Centurion recount what he had learned of the follower Judas, who had betrayed the Master. "Hung himself... In a potter's field. Hurled the silver coins before the priests in the Temple...the thirty pieces that the Sanhedrin had paid him for the betrayal. Poor fellow," he added.

"I too pity him," said Cleopas, now more sedate, seemingly having cleansed himself of an overwhelming agony. "I too betrayed him once," he moaned, "and like Judas, for money..."

Cornelius interrupted with a grunt. "Do not rehearse that again! Surely He has forgiven you. You said He looked into your eyes and smiled. You said that at that precise moment a wave of peace swept over you. What sign more do you seek than from God?"

"Yes. I must remember that." Cleopas mopped at his face as they hurried up the hill to the city. "Still, I have prayed for ten thousand days since that first lost opportunity in Bethlehem to have Him stay, even if for a moment, as a guest in my inn. I had hoped that he might grace the open door of my humble boarding home. You know, give him the room I had once denied him as a babe. Now...it is forever too late."

"It is said in ancient Hebrew text," Sam broke in at last as they neared the gate of Gennath, "that the dead shall rise from the grave." Hearing this, the other two stopped, frozen in their tracks, and eyed him questioningly.

Cleopas let out a short gasp and stared over at his mysterious new friend, his mouth agape, then asked, "You know Hebrew? You have read the scrolls of Ezekiel? Jeremiah? Isaiah? Job?"

"Yes, I have read a compendium of the scrolls," Sam answered.

"He, Jesus," Cornelius nodded, "prophesied that 'this temple shall be destroyed but raise the third day.' Some say it is his body he referred to. Others, the temple itself."

"No one understands that to mean anything but His spirit, surely," Cleopas returned, "just as all men's spirits go on."

Sam met the innkeeper's gaze. "He could have meant it literally, referring to the temple. But as a student and reporter of the human condition, I must add that He might have been speaking in figurative terms. Meaning his body, that is." Sam let his words sink in. He knew what his beloved Rachel believed. Clearly, these men believed in the divinity of Jesus. But, of course, they had seen him, witnessed certain things. But he, himself, refused to believe. Without seeing miracles for himself, or at least unearthing evidence of miracles, healings and such linked to the man Jesus, it was all supposition.

But now that he was somehow wrapped up in this historic - albeit dreamlike - frame of mind, he felt compelled to offer the possibility to his two fellow travelers, that the New Testament commentary of literal resurrection was a possibility.

The two men continued to glance over at him, lost in thought. Yet their countenances spoke volumes: they were acknowledging the plausibility of Jesus' literal resurrection.

"You speak as one having faith," Cleopas replied as they came within sight of Jerusalem. "You do not cease to amaze me, Samuel Antonius."

Sam merely shook off the idea. "Not faith, just interest in truth."

The Centurion drew a finger to his lips. "Let us be cautious now. There are many ears in this city, those all too anxious to play the informer for a mere shekel. False steps may give the enemies of those who followed the Master a doom too horrible to contemplate. Come, now, let us enter the gate and go quietly."

19

"IT IS FINISHED"

"This is where we part, for now, friend," the Centurion said, gripping the other's hand and forearm with his. "I must escort Samuel to the residence of the Procurator. I shall seek word of you at John Mark's soon. Go there."

"I shall. Then on the morrow you will return with me to Emmaus?" Cleopas asked, having found renewed sense of purpose and strength.

"Yes. I shall meet you at this gate at the sixth hour."

"Very well. Shalom, my friend," Cleopas saluted. "And peace be unto you, Samuel. I hope you find what you seek. You are welcome to return to my inn with us on the morrow."

"Shalom, Cleopas. I appreciate your hospitality. Will you be safe?" Sam's head tilted toward the figure of a man nearby.

"Being here, now, yes. The man in the shadows? That is one of the brethren, waiting to escort me," he said under his breath, gesturing toward a wall and alleyway ten meters to his left. The man nodded and motioned for Cleopas to join him. "I shall be safe, Samuel, and thank you for the concern. Forgive my pitiful and unmanly display of emotions. I have no excuse. I will gather strength once I reach John Mark's and find my wife Mary."

"No need to apologize. I understand," Sam replied.

"Remember your promise to me?" Cleopas asked, hinting of the Centurion's veiled friendship with the disciples. "And if we do not meet again, when you make your report, you will tell your world I did not refuse my Master the second time? Tell them that Cleopas, the innkeeper of Bethlehem and Emmaus, gave everything he had to the cause. And though failing, his intent and heart was full for Jesus of Nazareth... You will tell the world?"

Sam gave a nod. "Yes, I promise."

"God bless you, then," he offered, reaching out to grip Sam's forearms. "I will keep my promise to you as well," he weakly smiled. "Farewell, my brothers," he whispered as he slipped into the darkened side streets of Jerusalem in company of the stranger.

"Come, Samuel," the ruddy-complexioned soldier ordered.

They had walked but a few paces when Sam opened up. "You are a true friend. Uncommon. Very uncommon."

The Roman issued no response.

The Passover having ended, the Sabbath-day observances complete, the Jewish pilgrims were preparing for their departure to the many towns of Palestine, Judea, and Galilee. The Jerusalem residents, in turn, solemnly hushed with the going down of the sun, had settled their business this day. Heavy thoughts on the events that shook the city in the past three days occupied the vivid story-telling taking place behind closed doors and shuttered windows as the two made their way through deserted and silent streets.

Cornelius at last broke the stillness. "The city trembled yesterday. Sabbath eve. The ground quaked. A storm unlike any I have ever beheld overtook the very sun in the heavens. Blackened the sky. The day turned completely dark, as it now begins to be. But the hour was not yet evening."

"Such things happen," Sam responded.

"Yes, but this was no simple anomaly of weather. This happened precisely with the speaking of three words. I heard them; I was there."

"Where?"

"The hill of the skull. Golgotha, Jerusalemites call it."

"What where the words?" Sam queried, suddenly aware that a new, more intimate openness was emerging between him and the Roman soldier.

"It is finished," he replied solemnly.

"The words came from whom?"

"The Jew called Jesus."

"Did you participate in the crucifixion?"

"Fair question," the soldier groaned, his chin lowering to meet his chest. "Yes, and no. I refused Pilate's order to carry out the execution. I saw through it. My sympathies have been suspect for some time. Normally, I would have begged off under the pretense of illness. Instead, I commanded my subordinate, Quintus, to commence, then I had a plaque delivered. It was posted above the head of the martyred Master. Then, not being able to stay away, drawn somehow to the site, I was there when he gave up the ghost. By refusing to go directly and immediately to the execution site, I confirmed the suspicions of Pilate's main henchman Valerius, a Tribune of noble birth; one willing to do whatever it takes to rise in position and authority. His father knows my father. Though both senators, they are hardly friends."

"He a Tribune and you a Centurion?"

"Yes. I am adopted. All know it. I am Iberian of birth."

"That must make you feel – "

Cornelius cut him off mid-sentence. "Nothing! May they all be damned! I feel nothing! Do I need their honors? It is nothing but hollowness. Empty sounds reverberate from their chests as they pound upon them in their pride," he spit out disdainfully. "I know who I am. That is enough."

Sam was in his zone now. The interviewer asking tough questions, seeking raw emotions in order to expose the naked truth. "What did the wood plaque say?" he queried.

The soldier grunted something in Latin, then smiled. "Nice to win, now and then. A victory, of sorts. Valerius himself posted it above the Master, thinking to trap me. Ha!"

Sam nodded. He was fully aware of the words it contained. He'd seen the movie, the Hollywood version. "Pilate didn't mind?" he asked.

"No. It has been whispered that his soul is tormented. His wife Claudia came to him troubled by a dream, telling him to not 'lay a hand on this man.' Now he wished he hadn't, I can tell you. He wanted nothing to do with the scheming Sanhedrin, led by Caiaphas, the High Priest. Washed his hands of the whole matter. Made them assent to the death of the innocent man, by releasing a true criminal. One named Barrabas. At least I give him that."

"And Valerius?"

"Valerius is a proud man and a fool. He reminds me in both visage and manner of a dangerous animal, a weasel or badger, something with sharp eyes and equally sharp teeth. Watch yourself with that one," Cornelius added for emphasis.

"One false step, one move against Emperor Tiberius in word or deed, and he shall pave his path to the top upon your sun-bleached bones."

Sam considered the passion of the Roman and fell silent as the two wound their way down alleyways and streets. "The old city," he whispered.

"Not a word now," cautioned the Centurion, "not until we arrive at the Fortress."

If I am alive, I should be waking from the surgery soon, Sam thought. *Rachel*, he whispered. He thought of her now, and of her last words to him... *Be whole.*

20

TRIBUNE

"Announce us to Pilate's offices. Make haste, soldier." The order brought the guard to full readiness. "I have with me this man, librarian from the Senate who brings a message from Rome." With that, Cornelius turned and issued instructions for his men to report to their quarters. The guard saluted Centurion Cornelius and left him along with Sam at the entrance to the Procurator's palace, in company of another guard.

"I hope you have prepared your message from the Senate, Samuel Antonius."

Sam blinked and swallowed hard. He glanced around at the cold but stately surroundings. He sensed danger - even death - here. Legionnaires lined the outer perimeter. The gate was guarded closely. The crude laughter, a scream he thought he heard coming from inside, told him the place had also known much pain, as well: a dungeon, torture cells, perhaps a rough-hewn gallows.

"These soldiers are tested. Make no mistake, Samuel," Cornelius whispered. "With the cold blood of steel and iron running through their veins, these are men of battle, bearing bloodied weapons of war - spears, broad swords, shields - always expecting trouble, inflicting swift punishment to those who
oppose them. Not to be trifled with," he added for emphasis. "They protect the Emperor's governor, and even I, a recognized Centurion, must pass the test, the utter and complete scrutiny of these guards, if I am to enter these gates."

He was scourged here, Sam thought. He remembered the Christmas Devotional so many years before in Memphis; he had been the narrator, and his beloved Rachel a member of the Youth Symphony. Now he also recalled the innkeeper's biblical cry to Joseph and Mary: *"No room!"* - but until now he had never heard the innkeeper's lament. He'd witnessed the passion play of the Christ's final moments, the mocking of the Roman soldiers, but not once had he imagined the respect this Centurion paid.

Sam gazed at his Roman escort. Everything seemed so familiar. When his voice shifted from commanding and demanding, to quietly instructive, there was a quality he seemed to recognize, a milder characteristic to it. He admired the steadiness of the man, the utter contempt for worldly authority he calmly held close to him like a hand of cards well played, yet his simultaneous surrender to that same authority, using it now to meet his ends.

Some time passed before the guard returned. In his wake strode another man, a crimson tunic draped authoritatively over one shoulder. He strutted as he walked, wore brass breast-plate and symbols announcing, silently yet commandingly, that he was a high-ranking officer.

"Valerius himself," Cornelius whispered. "Guard your words."

"Centurion Cornelius. I would have thought you in Caesarea by now. But then you had a weak stomach yesterday." Valerius sized him up the way a hungry man might a slab of cooked meat. The insolent eye contact, the bold swagger, the verbal sparring, all in an attempt to raise from Cornelius some cross word. "And who have we here?" The question was not so much a question as a challenge.

"He presented his papers with your guard. You know who he is by now." Cornelius spared no words. Sam sensed that it was the only way to deal with such a man: direct, bold, yet plain.

"Yes. A librarian of the Senate. A soft man, one not accustomed to the harsh conditions of Palestine, I see. Well, the Procurator has retired. I shall see you both to the guest chambers." Then, to add a bit of salt to the wound he was in the process of inflicting, he added, speaking to Cornelius, "I assume that you have no problem staying in the same hall with a citizen; a civilian of Rome?"

"I understand it to be an honor."

"And a duty, Centurion," Valerius spat back. "We waste no manpower here on suspected spies. You brought him, you guard him. There has been enough intrigue this past week to last a year." He turned to the guard nearest him. "Escort them to the guest chambers," he commanded. "Lodging suitable for honored visitors of Rome."

The guard nodded for them to follow after him. "Samuel Antonius," Valerius called after them, his voice smooth as silk, "I hope you will excuse what may appear as rudeness. It is simply a matter of many duties to attend to."

"No need, Tribune Valerius," Sam replied.

"By your leave, then. Gentlemen, we shall expect you to break the fast with the Governor in the morning at the first hour. The day starts early. Good evening to you."

"And to you, Tribune," Sam indulged.

"By your leave, Tribune Valerius," Cornelius saluted.

Valerius nodded, turned, and then stopped once more. "Oh, by the way, Centurion," he called out. "The Governor was amused. Thought it would be something, a memento, shall we say?" He tossed an oblong, wooden object to the ground before Cornelius, its clatter echoing down the hall. "Hail the divine Tiberius." The Tribune offered the stiff hand salute.

The Centurion did not flinch, conspicuously refusing to offer the customary return of salute.

"I see," Valerius noted. "Well, then. You may have your God and King, Centurion. Yours is all a matter of time." He made sure to catch the eye of Centurion Cornelius, see the contempt in them, judge his adversary well.

"He does not like you," Sam whispered as the Tribune turned his back and walked away.

"Nor you. You did not return the salute, either," Cornelius noted, and reached down to retrieve the coarse plaque. He brushed at it as if wiping dust, dirt, or filth of any kind from it. Satisfied that it no longer bore a scintilla of Valerius's stench and stain, he held it up reverently before tucking it safely inside his leather satchel, hung from his waistband. "We must be still tonight. The guards will spy on us," he added.

Sam nodded, all too willing to sleep and be done with this drama, willing to awaken to Rachel's beautiful smile. He looked on as Cornelius finished concealing the inscribed wooden sign among the many documents, orders and other correspondence that filled the satchel. He had recognized three languages etched into the fir board. He did not understand the Hebrew and Greek, but he could plainly make out the third, the Latin: *Jesus of Nazareth– King of the Jews*

21

FORTRESS ANTONIA

The summons to attend the morning meal came early. Antonia Palace, situated within the walls of the Fortress Antonia, consisted of a series of corridors flanked by the traditional Grecian columns. It rose a mere one hundred meters from the sleeping quarters of the soldiers. Statues of a variety of appropriated Gods from the Greek and other cultures – and more than one bust of the various Caesars – lined the long halls interconnecting rooms designed for meetings, banquets, tribunals and entertainment.

Sam was awestruck with the majesty of Rome, manifest in the architectural and artistic perfection of integrated marble floors, columns, porticos, balustrades, and the fine plaster moldings that seamlessly blended to make this place a classic archetype of the Roman Empire. In fact, the edifice, it seemed, held a splendor and majesty separate from all other structures in the city.

All the movies I've seen wrapped into one... Ben Hur, Cleopatra, The Robe... *Magnificent!*

"Remember, Samuel, no more than the simplest answers," warned Cornelius in lowered voice, straightening his tunic. "You did well with Valerius last night. Now, after a good night's sleep, let us see if you can skillfully maneuver around your fellow Roman, the Procurator. But again, remember, you will find better reporting for your Senate with less talk and more listening."

"I've dealt with many politicians in my days of reporting. Indeed, you are quite right."

"Here we are," Cornelius quietly announced.

Valerius appeared at a set of double-entry doors opening to an elaborately appointed dining hall. Awaiting within were a rectangular table with mirror-polished marble slab, silver dining ware, and seats arranged for six. Valerius motioned for them to enter. "A sound sleep, gentlemen of Rome?" he inquired, nodding toward Sam.

"Yes, Tribune. Quite sound," Sam lied.

"Well, then, I assume our brave Centurion is rested enough today to see to the Procurator's requests...." He raised an eyebrow toward Cornelius.

"I and my men are always at the command of the Procurator," Cornelius curtly announced.

"Seems you hesitated to take charge of the crucifixion," blurted Valerius, cocking his head to one side and adding, "upon the Procurator's order, at that. I believe he may have a word or two for you in that respect." Pilate and his wife had not yet arrived. The Tribune was probing his adversary, but stabbing at Cornelius as well, seeking to throw him off balance, cause the man to stumble or lose control of his emotions.

"I was there," Cornelius unflinchingly announced.

"Ah, yes. After the awful business had already commenced. You do admire this dead man, Jesus of Nazareth, don't you, Centurion?"

Cornelius's mind raced to summon what he might say. Simultaneously, it harkened back to that fateful hour just two days earlier. In seconds he recalled it all: the order, his anger, his reaction...

22

THE CENTURION'S CHOICE

<u>Two Days Ago</u>

"You are to personally carry out the execution of this Jewish troublemaker, Centurion Cornelius. Here are your orders, direct from the Procurator, I might add." Valerius sneered, well aware of the man's admiration for the Jews and, in particular, this condemned Jesus of Nazareth.

Cornelius tucked the order away, saluted and turned.

"Yes, see to it, Centurion," the Tribune called after him. "I will be watching and reporting to Pilate. See that you do not disappoint me."

With Valerius's departure, Cornelius sought out his second in command and handed him the written charge. "See to it, Quintus," he instructed softly. "And hasten this man's death that he might not suffer." Then, before Quintus could take his leave, the commander once more addressed his duties. "Quintus," he added. The man came to attention. "Take your time in route to the place of execution. I have a matter to conduct. I am quite ill and have suffered greatly this past week. You have been a witness to my condition?" he asked, with his eyes as much as with his voice.

"Aye, Centurion, sir. I have been a witness."

"Good. Now go. I will refrain from being at hand during the nailing. See to it. I will come as quickly as I gain command over my sickness."

Quintus saluted and exited to call his men to their task. Now feigning ill, Cornelius, though he trod a bit slower, went directly to the carpenter's repair room, which occupied a remote corner of the fortress compound. A slab of fresh-cut fir caught his attention the minute he entered. It rested upon a bench as if destined for this purpose.

"Carpenter!" he called out. A local craftsman who worked for the Roman garrison appeared.

"Prepare me a sign. Upon the orders of Pontius Pilate, Governor and Procurator of Rome."

"Yes, master. What shall I inscribe?"

"Inscribe the following..." Taking a lead marker, he then lightly scratched the caption into the hard-baked clay ground outside the carpenter's door, words in Hebrew, Greek and Latin.

"All three languages?"

"Yes."

It took but a few minutes for the craftsman to finish the job, whereupon Cornelius commanded, "Wax!"

The man dripped a portion of sealing wax on the back of the plaque, onto which, using his ring, the Centurion stamped the Roman emblem of the Cornelius family, an official seal his men would recognize. Then, with a ink quill and crimson tincture he offered a brief message next to his wax seal and charged the worker to deliver the etched board to Quintus.

The command on the back was clear: *Post above the man, by order*, it read. "Do not delay, carpenter. And, for your trouble," he finished, tossing the laborer a silver coin. "Hurry! Go! Another carpenter awaits," he glumly added under his breath.

The man hurried off down the street. Cornelius lagged behind, tormented by a mixture of guilt, abhorrence, fear, and torn allegiance. Finally, he began his long – and deliberately slow – journey through the narrow streets, on his way to Golgotha.

23

PILATE SPEAKS

"Centurion! Did I make myself clear? You do admire this dead man of Nazareth, don't you?" Valerius scoffed.

"As the words on the plaque were inscribed," Cornelius answered, awakening his mind from his reverie to the present danger.

"Well, here comes our Governor now," Valerius noted, eyeing the far wing of the dining hall. "Hail, Caesar Tiberius, the only King, and his Governor, the most excellent Pontius Pilate!" the Tribune announced.

"Yes, yes. Hail to all," Pilate responded, clearly in no mood for formalities. A chill ran up Sam's back upon first sight of the man. Indeed, a solemn, dark cloud seemed to follow him. He appeared nervous, agitated. His eyes flitted from face to face, only pausing long enough to lock a stern scowl on each pair of eyes. He took his place at the head of the table and motioned for the others to be seated.

"Who have we today?" he asked coolly, his gaze fixed upon the still-empty bowl set before him.

"The Centurion Cornelius has escorted one Samuel Antonius from the Senate Library to your Palace, your Excellency."

"And what business does citizen Antonius bring from Rome?"

"He brings no apparent business, sir, but is an *observer*," reported Valerius, the dead weight of the latter word catching in his throat as if a shred of rotting meat.

The victuals arrived. Pilate paid them no mind, but continued his duel of words. "Ah, an observer. Well, then, I hope he *observed* scrupulously the events of the past two days." With that, he squinted, then set to rotating his head, his neck acting as a fulcrum. "Couldn't sleep," he mewed to no one in particular. "Haven't had an appetite. I must have the illness contracted by our intrepid Centurion...."

Tribune Valerius glared over at Cornelius, a smirk written upon his face, clearly pleased that Pilate had already presented the issue of Cornelius's failure the hour of the Nazarene's execution.

"Well, then, names?"

"Samuel Antonius," the Tribune announced.

"Alone? No assistant?" Pilate asked, motioning to the servers to take away food with which he, at the moment, happened to be annoyed.

"I come alone, Governor Pilate. I bring greetings."

"Yes, I am sure you do," he muttered, his words like ice. Then, without so much as shifting in his seat, he addressed Cornelius. "And how did you happen upon this man, Centurion?"

"On the road."

"Alone?"

"Yes, sire."

"Strange."

"Yes, sire."

Again Pilate's questioning turned to Sam, though his full attention seemed focused on the platter of assorted fruit set before him. "How is it that you are found traveling, alone, on the road to Jerusalem from Caesarea, Samuel Antonius?" Then, as if he had suddenly remembered his manners, he exclaimed, motioning to the others, "Eat, eat!"

"I did not come alone, not entirely," Sam began, not sure where his comment was leading, "But I am pleased to say..." he stammered.

Just then Pilate's wife entered. Sam sighed in relief as the ashen, obviously shaken woman hurried to his side and spoke openly for all to hear. "Did I not *tell* you! Did I not *warn* you!" she shrieked. "It has come to pass. Now all is lost. You will hear from Tiberius himself. What shall we do?"

Pilate became instantly agitated by the commotion. "Get control, woman! Of what news do you speak?" he roared.

"The High Priest. He waits. Oh, if you had seen my dream. Our fate is sealed! Now we will suffer for condemning the just Galilean!" she lamented.

Pilate's patience was already worn thin. His mind had been plagued by the affair ever since its climax two days earlier. Now his own culpability in the matter had reached its zenith. "*Ecce homo*! I said to the crowd. *Ecce homo*! *Behold the man*! The man in whom I find no guilt! I told them. I...I did not...condemn...HIM! I washed my hands!" he shouted, now standing, pacing, his eyes scanning the courtyard below. "The rabble! The damnable mob! They demanded it for their God! The High Priest brought him condemned already...for treason, they said. For blaspheme, they claimed! Claudia, by all the Gods of Rome, I swear, I did not condemn Jesus of Nazareth!"

The Governor was trembling now, nervous glances darting about the room. For his part, Valerius was taking in this scene, this marvelous turn of events, with cautious delight. He saw through the Governor's thin-skinned bravado. Pilate's weakness would buckle under Valerius's lust for power. For years Valerius had coveted the governorship. Now his meticulous scheming would pay off. He felt sure his time was soon at hand.

"Well? Where is Caiaphas?" he barked. "Cannot a man get a portion of food to start his day before these people bring their problems to me? Tribune!"

"Yes sire. I will see to it." Valerius stood, bowed, and discreetly exited the room.

"You see, Samuel Antonius, what I have to deal with? You may tell the Senate. Tell them that the Governor barely rises in the morning and cannot take a morsel of food for nourishment. Rather, he must attend to the demands of the Jewish leaders in order to keep peace in this part of the Empire. Note it well. Tell them, *scribe*."

Pilate once more assumed his seat at the head of the table. "Sit, Claudia," he commanded. Then, lowering his tone to a near whisper, he croaked, "Let us act the part, dear one. Let not this man destroy your peace nor see you in despair."

The woman gave a sigh, an attempt to breathe out the pent-up fears. Then, somewhat mollified, she took her place next to him

"Uh, hem...ah sire," Valerius whispered. "Caiaphas demands an audience at once. It seems the body of the Nazarene...is missing."

Cornelius sat up, alert, solemn.

Sam, too, started at the news. He was familiar with this scene - the movie version, mostly. *Next comes Caiaphas,* he thought to himself.

Pilate stood and slammed his hands down upon the table, causing it to quake under his blow. "You posted the guards!" he bellowed, pointing a trembling finger at his aide. "*You,* Tribune! I suggest *you* find these men! The punishment is death, Tribune," he hissed, his face red with rage. "You know this? Do you?"

Valerius was now at a loss for words, seemingly stunned by the abrupt change of events. He backed away. "At once. I will seek them at once," he whimpered, wasting no small effort to maintain his dignity.

"And send the fattened overseer of the Temple treasury to me!" Pilate added with contempt and force enough for anyone in the palace to hear.

"Yes, sire," the sniveling aristocrat answered as he made a hasty retreat from the dining room.

"These people and their Gods!" Pilate growled while half-heartedly poking a morsel of flat bread into his mouth and again taking his seat. "Our Gods are sensible. Correct me if I am wrong, guest Antonius, but our Gods simply do not get in the way! Is that not so? When was the last time a God of Rome created a scandal? Hum?"

Sam, summoning all the diplomatic tact he'd garnered over four decades of reporting, sought to appease the fiery interviewee seated before him. "Roman Gods indeed do not get in the way. Quite convenient, really," he said. In truth, he was rather enjoying the pageant being presented to him. *The best performance I've ever seen,* he thought silently, contemplating the visual spectacle of the Easter story his mind was witnessing while his body slept.

"Yes, yes! Convenient Gods! And that is the wisdom and greatness of Rome — convenience! We do things with the end in mind, for the peace and prosperity of the Empire. I once brought shields to the temple, shields upon which the Roman eagle was emblazoned in tribute to the *divine* Tiberius. I marched them through Jerusalem, and you would think I was starting the city ablaze! The uproar! Ha!" He paused to spit, expelling in proxy a trace of the bitterness awash inside him. "Chastised by Tiberius himself, I finally took them down and stored them. The eagle! The Jewish leaders said it was sacrilege, mind you. Ha!"

Claudia fidgeted. Her raw nerves had reduced her to a sullen and tearful hostess of Rome.

"So *that* is why you are here!" Pilate accused, his ire directed at Sam. He stood and approached his puzzling guest. Both Sam and Cornelius countered by respectfully standing. "You are here to spy for Tiberius, hum?" he alleged, passing his hand across a strong, clean-shaven jaw. He stopped, once more pondering where all this might lead, postulating further upon the impossible nature of his governance of such a people, rambling on about power struggles within the court.

In self-talk, Pilate began again. "If I am correct, Tiberius has heard of this enchanted man, this Jesus. I, of course, had him killed. Against my will, mind you." He made a point of repeating it for the Senate Librarian. "Against my will! But then, how would Tiberius know that?" he inquired to no one in particular. "Well, no matter. I did it," he glumly concluded. "In the end, I will be blamed. And all to satisfy the bloodlust of the mob. So Tiberius would have had me do...what? Send the magic man to Rome, where he could then heal Tiberius of his infirmities? Would he himself then act as judge, whether the man be a traitor, a threat to Rome?"

Pilate turned to face Sam. "I have never heard of you before. No one enters Palestine from the seaport or by land from Rome without my knowledge. So...you may be more dangerous than a spy. Here to replace me, perhaps? No...not even Tiberius would allow anything but a grand entry for the next Governor, his divine representative." He stopped, strolled a few paces. "Then who are you, Samuel, man with the Hebrew given name and Roman surname?" Pilate allowed for the silence, even as shouting in Aramaic could be heard from the anteroom without the dining hall.

"Sire," Valerius announced, almost stumbling through the doorway. "I beg your pardon, sire. It does appear the Jew, Caiaphas the High Priest, requires your Excellency's presence."

"Well, Samuel. Perhaps you would like to report this." He motioned for him to follow, but for Cornelius to stay. "No, on second thought, I will require your services as well, Centurion. Come!"

Claudia, fretting and mentally exhausted, followed, keeping a respectful distance. She needed to be nearby, needed whatever new information she could glean, needed somehow to regain her former sense of sanity.

"Your Highness, Governor Pilate. It is early. I beg your forgiveness for this intrusion. I..."

The Procurator cut him off. "Do you never weary of intrigue, Joseph Caiaphas?"

"It is not intrigue I seek. Quite the opposite. I seek the peace of the people, for the Empire's sake."

"Ha! Your own skin and the bags of money you have stashed in the cushions where you sit your well-fed, amply robed body! For the Empire's sake, indeed! You care nothing for the Empire. So, get on with it!" he tersely returned.

"We have suffered a humiliation. I take full blame. The guards you sent must simply have been overworked. They apparently slept and..."

You paid them off, Sam thought. *Last chapter in the Gospel of John.* He looked to Cornelius, who was on edge now, taking in every carefully chosen word.

"So the followers of this Jesus have stolen his body," continued Caiaphas. "It is your duty to find these men and have them imprisoned... Better yet, they shall stand trial and be put to the same treasonous end that the false prophet was."

"No, Caiaphas. I will not allow you to do your dirty work through me. If they merit stoning, do it. But never again will I allow your midnight courts of justice to use the Roman Empire as tools to dispose of dogmatic preachers you deem troublemakers. Never!"

Caiaphas shuffled his feet, but kept a firm gaze on Pilate. "With all due respect for the bother I have caused you and having acknowledged the part I have played in it, I must insist we bring a swift hand to remedy this matter. You see, Governor, this dead man Jesus claimed to be the Son of God, capable of raising the dead! His followers mock you, and me," he whined. "They have taken his body, no doubt buried it in an unmarked grave, and now will shout throughout all Palestine that he, Jesus of Nazareth, has risen; has come back from the dead!"

"With his body? His dead, crucified body?" Pilate asked, incredulous. "The people you claim to lead will believe such utter nonsense?"

"It is not nonsense to them. They are unwavering in their belief. There has been more than one purported 'miracle' of raising others from the dead. His friend, Lazarus of Bethany, is one such story. Many witnesses claim...but it is all a matter of publicity for their own cause," he said. "So you see, these followers *are* dangerous!"

"I would not want to be your enemy, Caiaphas. It is you who is dangerous," Pilate stated directly as he paced a circle around the man. "What say you, Samuel Antonius?"

Sam looked to Cornelius, who evinced no sign of facial expression nor distinguishable body language to tell Sam how to respond. He remained stiff, eyes to the front, but fixed with contempt for the High Priest.

Sam then nodded toward Caiaphas. "May I ask of this man, your High Priest, a few pointed questions?"

"Most certainly," Pilate said, lips biting down hard in scorn. "Ask anything you like."

"Governor Pilate," pled the pious High Priest, a nervous rise in his voice. "I beseech you, there is little time to waste. And who is this man to ask questions of me?"

"He is a Roman! And I will have your tongue cut out, leader of your people or not, next time you dare question my judgment! Centurion!"

Cornelius came forward, his hand on the hilt of his broadsword.

Caiaphas turned away from the brawny soldier and bowed his head before Sam. Through pursed lips he disdainfully said, "Please, ask anything you wish."

Sam's nod sent Cornelius's sword back into its sheath. Drawing a cleansing breath, Sam took his place before Caiaphas. "Jesus of Nazareth was tried at night, was he not?" he asked.

"Yes, but..."

"And that is strictly forbidden by Jewish law, is it not?"

"There are cases that..."

"No, there are not. None, in fact. This was a first. Certainly during your rule, yes?" The blaze that was lit in Sam's eyes bore into the Priest's. "Well?"

"Yes," Caiaphas finally answered. "But there were circumstances which..."

"None of that!" Pilate bellowed. "We've already endured your litany of why the man was a blasphemer and a traitor. Just answer with *yea* or *nay,* Caiaphas!"

Sam continued. "And you are required to conduct a trial before the Sanhedrin?"

"Members were present."

"But not all, and not in the chambers of the Sanhedrin, but in your own house. Is that not so?"

"Yes. But I am the High Priest. In my words and those of the council reside the law," he spat back.

"So it was a covert trial, and Jewish law honors the public nature, the daylight nature, the presumptive innocence of a man under condemnation and arrest. Yea or nay?"

Caiaphas fell silent.

"How is it that in your words of law no court should be convened but in public and not before the morning sacrifice, and must end by evening sacrifice. Yet this tribunal of the condemned Jesus was held, I'll repeat it once again, *after* the evening sacrifice, and hardly public."

"Citizens were present," he countered. "In fact, two of the condemned's followers were reported there."

"No death sentence may be pronounced without a defender at hand. Unanimous consent for capital punishment on the same day of the trial, and without representation, is tantamount to acquittal. Is it not so?"

"In some areas you seem knowledgeable. I am amazed at your familiarity with Jewish law. May I ask your name and profession, sir?" Caiaphas diplomatically rejoined.

"Samuel Antonius. I am a reporter."

"Oh, reporter now is a profession?" the High Priest mocked. "I see..."

"'They shall not judge on the eve of a Sabbath, nor on that of any festival.' That is found in your Mishna. It is you who is guilty of a crime, sir." He paused and stepped back, allowing the High Priest his answer. Sam had recalled without seeming exertion the words of an interview he had done the year before. He'd felt compelled to read the entire book before the interview. Now its pages were brought to mind effortlessly, word for word. *The Illegal Trial of Jesus – From A Jurist's Bench*, by Supreme Court Justice David Broadbent, had been released that first week in December and been on the bestseller charts for four months running.

When next Sam's gaze met that of the High Priest, Caiaphas had closed his eyes and gritted his teeth, seething. Clenched fists clutched tightly at his side, and his face explosive with rage, he turned to Pilate and cried, "Do not listen to this man!"

"The deed is done, Caiaphas. Would that I could raise Jesus myself from the dead just to see your face," returned the other, grinning in contempt.

Valerius had purposely stepped back from the fray, taking in all the political ramifications of this event. Knowing he was ultimately accountable for the guards, he attempted now to remedy the defect by taking the offensive and regaining Pilate's confidence. "I have taken the guards into custody, sire. They will be punished according to law. They are in chains already, and bound for the salt pits in lower Judea. What better form of death than this?"

Pilate waved him off, instantly seeing through the nonsense.

Caiaphas, though remaining mute, questioned this new information with his eyes. He, himself, had paid them handsomely – had sent them east in clothing and with documents of the court so that they would not be recognized. He had even allowed them ten years' legionnaire pay and a yearly stipend for their silence. If Valerius had in truth intercepted them, however, there could be trouble.

"Let us conclude the matter," the High Priest at last put forward, in a last-ditch effort to sway Pilate. "You have need for peace, an end to rebellion. I have need for peace, and an end to heretics." Then he ended his remarks by flashing a sneering gaze in Sam's direction and saying, "I hope your stay is a short and pleasant one, *reporter* Samuel Antonius."

"Tribune Valerius," commanded Pilate, "see to this man's complaint, then bring the guards to me."

"I shall, your Excellency. I have charged the Centurion's band with their security." He smiled, bowed, and gave a cunning glance in Cornelius's direction.

Cornelius nodded, imparting no hint of fear. Whether Valerius's story was true or false, he knew that, for now, at least, the man had him clearly in his sights. If he lied, Valerius could charge Quintus and those under him with dereliction of duty and, by way of default, he, Cornelius, would fall. But if Quintus indeed still had the men in his charge, then he, Cornelius, was safe. The Centurion sensed it was the latter. Quintus was the best; a match for ten men.

"Good day, your Excellency," Caiaphas purred as he followed Valerius out of the room, pleased that he had the Tribune, assistant to the Procurator himself, to turn on to the followers of Jesus.

Cornelius now ventured to speak. "Sire?"

"Speak, Centurion," Pilate ordered as he returned to the table to sit with his wife, who, though forlorn and under considerable anxiety, had taken in the proceedings with interest.

Cornelius, unflustered by the recent turn of events, spoke boldly. "With due respect, sire, I am unsure how Valerius could find the missing guards, put them in my care, and all this only moments before you, yourself, found out about their failings at their post. With respect for the Tribune, of course."

Pontius Pilate smiled. He rubbed at his eyes and sought to comfort Claudia, her hands wrapped in his as she quietly sobbed. "I have not risen through the ranks for being a fool, Centurion. I will deal with Valerius myself." He stood, stretched, parted the shear lace curtains with one hand and gazed out to the courtyard below, now bustling with soldiers. "That is, if Rome does not deal with me first," he mumbled to himself.

Cornelius came to Pilate's defense. "I am your witness, sire. You tried to do justice. I will testify to that."

"Yes, yes. Well, you are a man of your word. I have no doubts. Your adopted family is well known for its integrity. So I will charge you with this: Take this man away from here before he falls into the wrong hands. Caiaphas has guards of his own. People disappear. Do you understand me?"

"Indeed, sire," Cornelius replied. "And what of the followers, sire, if you do not mind my asking?"

Pilate turned. "I know of your good intentions, Centurion. I know also about the so-called miracle."

Cornelius flashed him a questioning look.

"Yes, of your servant. That this Jesus healed him, restoring him to full health in a single touch. Stories such as this cannot help your advancement and should not get back to Rome. Anyway, I do not believe in the superstitious. It was fate that healed your servant, not faith. However, my men are free to believe as they will. One additional God for Rome cannot hurt. But I warn you, Centurion, do not put yourself beyond my reach to help you. Take care with these so called disciples, these followers of the crucified Jesus, that the net which is cast to trap them does not snare you as well. Do you understand?"

"Yes, sire. I understand."

"And as for you, Samuel Antonius," Pilate uttered in soft but all too cautionary tones, "you are not all you pretend to be. You defied Caiaphas. You played the advocate for a dead man you do not even know. You appear on the second morn after his death and pretend to have never been here, to have known nothing, to have come direct from Rome. You, sir, are more than you say you are. I would admonish you to keep this business to yourself as I inquire further about you... Leave me! My head aches from all this foolishness."

Cornelius snapped a salute. Pilate sunk back into the cushioned chair near his wife. Sam bowed respectfully and followed Cornelius out the way they had come.

"Centurion Cornelius," Pilate called as they reached the door. "Fear nothing of Valerius. Yes, I know of his schemes against you. You won the moment you delivered the plaque and had it posted on the Nazarene's cross at Golgotha."

Cornelius bowed slightly. "Thank you, sire. Come Samuel."

24

THE VOICE

Cornelius had now officially been given guardianship over this Samuel Antonius. In truth, he wished the man would simply go away. He had neither the time nor the energy to trouble himself with the soft man, the stranger who had appeared from nowhere to stir up Valerius even more against him.

He, Cornelius, just wanted his life back. He didn't fancy this sort of intrigue. His wife, Rebekkah of Tyre, was the jewel in his crown – the crown of a king in his own home, the only crown or glory he had ever sought. Alas, their union had been childless. He would have done anything to have offspring, to know the joy of fathering children. And, indeed, the most beautiful babies would have issued from her womb.

At one time, he had entertained the thought that inasmuch as the Master had healed his servant, that he might invite Him to his home on the coast one day, and there see his wife blessed. She had not been a believer until that day Jahath was raised from his deathbed. Jahath was a slave, a servant granted him of his adopted father, the Senator. But to Cornelius, Jahath was his best of friends, an equal who one day would have his papers made up, granting him his freedom.

So on that day Rebekkah had seen with her own eyes the workings of the Nazarene, and had begun listening to the story of the how Jesus of Galilee preached words of peace, kindness, brotherhood for all mankind, and did miracles only a prophet could do. Soon he, Cornelius, would be back in her embrace, and he would personally tell her of the awful events, how he had removed Jesus tenderly from the cross, had turned the body over to the merchant Joseph of Arimathea, kin to Mary, his mother. He recalled the words that so spontaneously poured from the Savior's lips moments before His death. The sky had blackened, the earth had shook to its center, thunder had roiled in the heavens and lighting had sent its tentacle arms across the starless firmament. He was standing next to Quintus, his right hand in the business of that day.

The crucified one had groaned and called out simply, "*It is finished!*" then given up the ghost.

Cornelius was strangely aware at that moment that, for him and his household, "it" had really just begun. "Truly, this man was the Son of God," he had unashamedly uttered.

For that spoken declaration and for the words carved upon the plaque, he would have to deal with the suspicious and ladder-climbing Valerius. He turned his attention now to Samuel as they exited the Fortress. "You presented yourself like a lawyer of the court. How did you know about the events of the Passover eve?"

"I am a student, an observer by nature. I have sources."

"Well, you must have some faith in the Master, or you wouldn't have been so adversarial with Caiaphas. It is not safe for you now," intoned Cornelius.

"I wish I could go home," Sam lamented as they proceeded toward an upper room where Cornelius had determined to go.

"Your wife? She does not travel with you?"

"Not on this trip. We were to leave for vacation on some islands, when I suffered a heart attack."

"Your heart is not well?"

"No. I'm not sure it will ever be well. I just need to get through this now and wake up seeing Rachel."

"You must have faith, Samuel. If you believed, as I do now, in God's power, you would be healed."

"You really believe that?"

"I have seen it with my own two eyes and have had dozens of reports verified by those who were supposed to have been healed. None flinched at a Roman officer's interrogation."

"That does say something," Sam answered.

"Indeed. But you are the intellectual sort who must see to believe," Cornelius answered back, resting his fingertips next to his eyes.

"How else?"

"Faith comes expressly *before* the miracle, else why call it faith? The Master taught that very tenet and paid me an honor I shall always hold dear," explained

Cornelius. "He said, *'Such great faith I have not seen, no not in all of Israel.'* I have never forgotten that. He changed me. Then and there, the coarse, crude skeptic of Rome became the willing student, the open believer."

Sam let out a sigh. "My wife believes like you do. Always talking about how I'm not a *whole* person without God."

"So she has heard of our Lord already?"

"The word gets around," Sam answered.

"My wife is Rebekkah. I dream every night that she sleeps in my arms. I long to wake every day with her," the sturdy Roman wistfully replied. "Your wife? She did not travel with you to Palestine?"

Sam shook his head.

"You cannot talk of it. Well, I understand. I will leave you alone in the matter. I am taking you to the followers. Cleopas should be there, waiting, with answers regarding the body of Jesus."

Sam's curiosity spilled over concerning one matter: "Why do they call you *the friend*?" he asked.

"I requested the moniker. It is a distinct honor used by Jews everywhere for a Gentile who protects and defends them. I cannot divulge my loyalties, although Pilate and Valerius have me correctly divined. But still, if I am not known by name, I have no accusers. I am a deliveryman for the Empire. I transport goods safely with my one hundred soldiers across roads thieves roam. As such, I felt I could benefit my Jewish brothers and carry messages between cities for them as well. I cannot hope to be one with them in the faith - not really. I am not a Jew by birthright. But then...with the prophet dead, it avails little."

"A *friend* is *one* in faith. I have many Jewish friends at home. We are known as you and I know each other. Perceive a man as a brother and he is your brother, simple as that," Sam found himself adding.

"Wise," nodded the Centurion. "Good words. You are a strange man and Pilate is correct. You are more than what you have claimed to be, Samuel Antonius." They turned a corner. "Here, through this alley," motioned Cornelius. "It will offer a shorter route. Along here we shall find believers if we need them. Let us be silent now."

The hush of their route was punctuated only by the closing of window shutters, the cackle of hens, the occasional barking of a dog, the cries of children within the walls on either side of them. They now ventured into the back streets of any number of middle-east cities Sam might have seen featured in a *National Geographic* TV Special.

Sam was first to break the silence. "Who took the body?" he asked.

Cornelius wanted the truth as much as any man regarding the burial of Jesus. Why had the guards left their posts? Where would the body have been taken? And by whom? He flashed Sam a brief scowl of disapproval and said under muffled breath, "That is what we are going to find out."

"Halt!" a commanding voiced rang out from behind them as they passed through one of several shadowy passageways.

Cornelius spun around, drew his sword and posted himself in front of Sam. Men with spears appeared at both ends of the narrow walkway, a Roman at the lead of the group farthest from the two travelers.

"Valerius! What goes here?" called Cornelius.

"On a hunt for traitors! Perhaps you, Centurion!"

"Make your case quickly, Tribune, or let us pass. I am on business for Pilate."

"So, escorting a spy for the Senate is an errand for Pilate?"

"Make your case known or let us pass," repeated Cornelius. "Here," he said to Sam, withdrawing a dagger from his belt and offering Sam its hilt. "You may need this."

Sam took hold of the slender, silvery blade. The closest he had ever come to using a knife was the previous year while carving the Thanksgiving turkey – and even then, he had bungled the job. He doubted if he had the ability to use it. Frightened now, Sam didn't understand how, amid this crazy, meandering dreamscape, he had come to feel this emotion.

"Yes, I believe I will make my case," Valerius continued. "One, you are a supporter of this Jesus and his followers. Two, you conspired with the man's supporters to bribe the guards, who, under your authority, left their posts at the dead man's sepulcher. Three, you and this man," he uttered with contempt, pointing to

Sam, "are headed to warn the followers even now, so that they might make their escape."

The Tribune approached, broadsword drawn.

"Be sure you know how to use it, Valerius," Cornelius mocked.

On Valerius's signal, the guards from either end of the dark alleyway crept forward, effectively fencing in Cornelius and Sam, inch by inch.

"I am warning you, Tribune. I am on official business. You will answer to Pilate."

"Really? And what will I answer for? Let us see.... Centurion Cornelius is nowhere to be found. It is rumored he disappeared with the guards who abandoned their posts. It is rumored that the followers of this Jesus bought him off as well. Joseph of Arimathea is a wealthy man, after all. He provided the tomb. How convenient. It could have happened." He glared at his adversary, now at the distance of sword tips. "But then, with you and this Roman imposter here gone, this will all blow over rather quickly."

"Strike first, Valerius. I beg you. Strike," Cornelius answered. He knew some of the guards. Knew they would side with the winner of this contest - if nothing else, to save their own skins.

"You keep bad company, Centurion. You are a threat to Rome, as well. I have checked. There is no Samuel Antonius, Librarian of the Senate! And for treachery," he growled, "you both shall pay!" Walled in and with little room to shift from side to side, Valerius raised his sword high over his head, but not before the Centurion took advantage.

Cornelius was already positioned with his sword held at a right angle from his body. Tip pointed to Valerius's midsection, it was simple matter to lunge and disembowel the arrogant Tribune before his sword came down. But that would cause his father harm in Rome. One powerful Senator's son killing another's? No, Valerius would need to live this day, if at all possible.

As if on instinct, he employed a trick he recalled from his training days as a cadet in the Legion's Officer Corps: lunge between the legs, bring the sword up, and dissect - that is, slice the main artery in the upper thigh. No man alive will continue the fight, but will either beg for mercy or bleed to death.

The soldier's sword found its mark with sudden and startling force. Valerius froze mid-swing, his own sword still held aloft. Stunned, his face revealed his instant agony and vulnerability.

"How would you like to be remembered, Valerius?" derided Cornelius, the tip of his sword pressed up against the man's lower groin, its broadside angled at forty-five degrees. Disinclined to waste precious seconds with talk, he thrust it forward a bit, drawing a trickle of blood from the inner left thigh – a flesh wound, but nonetheless convincing. "Hum? You still a man, Valerius?"

At last, one of the guards could contain himself no longer. He let out a muffled guffaw, followed by another, until the hooting and hollering from the two Roman squads echoed up and down the passageway.

Cornelius, however, yet felt at risk. "Tell them to back off," he snarled, "or I will make you sorry you ever thought of raising the sword against me!"

The Tribune's eyes widened. He quickly considered the cold intent of the Centurion, hoping to come across some way to save face.

Cornelius intensified the upward pressure of his blade. "Drop the sword. Or would you rather I move mine? Just a bit to one side and I slice your main artery; up and to the right and I ruin your aspirations for progeny. You may die here now, Valerius. Do you think these," he said with a subtle sweep of his off hand in front of the guards both in front and back, "care who wins? They go with the one who walks away. Drop the sword or I swear I shall..."

Valerius straightway let his sword fall from his hand, sending it clattering to the hard-baked earth.

"Now, order them to retreat."

"Retreat. To your posts," Valerius squealed. The soldiers, still trying to confine the humor they'd found in Cornelius's gambit, retreated and soon disappeared.

"Samuel!" he called. "Retrace your steps to the nearest door behind you. Knock, offer them coins for silence, and wait for me."

Sam, just then regaining an awareness of all that had transpired in the previous few minutes, obeyed. Knocking, he found himself suddenly entering a dark room, three women peering at him from behind veiled faces. Dropping the dagger he yet clutched, he stretched out his hand toward them, offering up a handful of coins taken from the purse attached to his belt. The women backed away, huddling in one corner. With the door slightly ajar, he gazed back out into the narrow alleyway to the scene being played out.

"Now, Tribune, it is I who will dispatch you!" he heard his Centurion friend say angrily. "And you will be the man accused of this rebellion of the guards. It is you whose bones will be scattered upon the sands of the desert after dogs have feasted upon your worm-eaten flesh. You have met the match of your life, Tribune Valerius. Where are the witnesses? Where did they go? Hum?"

Valerius's face registered the shock and dread of a man about to meet a certain and ignominious death. Cornelius was caught up in a rage. He had been attacked. And now he was in a position he might never again know: an opportunity, and a just one at that, to do away with his tormentor. The weight from possible consequences was lost to him now as he let the tip of his weapon wander up and down Valerius's leg, pressing ever harder, enjoying the spectacle of his squirming enemy.

"Friend?"

The voice came from beyond Valerius, from the eastern end of the ally. The silhouette of a man at the end of the shadowy corridor caused him to pause. Maintaining the sword's pressure against the inner thigh of the Tribune, Cornelius stole a brief glance past his adversary in the direction of the shadowy figure. The man's voice rang out once more, a most pleasant voice.

"Cornelius..."

"I know that voice," he whispered.

Cornelius relaxed the pressure put to the sword. His face lightened. He did indeed recognize the voice! He had heard it before, more than enough to understand what it demanded of him. And the last time its calming influence had graced his ears had been but two days before – there, on the hill, at the place of the skull.

"Cornelius. Follow me."

The awestruck Centurion withdrew the sword, pointed Valerius in the opposite direction, nudged him on his way, and struck out for the voice, and the light.

25

THE WOMEN

"I mean no harm," Sam said to the terrified women crouching in the corner. "I will leave these coins here for you."

Cornelius knocked, then pushed the door open all the way. "Samuel. Make haste. We go to find Cleopas, and—"

"Centurion? Is that you?" one of the women cried out.

"Mary? Is that the voice of Mary of Emmaus?" he answered with surprise. "I knew some of the women followers lived nearby. But how? Why are you...?

"Is my Cleopas safe? Alive?" she asked as she stood and emerged into the light of the open door. "So many things have happened. So much in so little time!"

"He is," he said softly, kindly. "Cleopas is well. Mary, what are you doing here? I thought you were with the mother and the other Mary of Magdala."

Sam wondered at the spectacle. One minute a Roman bent on slaughtering his adversary, the next a mild gentleman determined to save and protect innocent friends.

"Did you see him?" Mary asked.

Another came forward. "Yes, did you see him? He appeared to us. At first we thought it a ghost."

"Joanna! And Salome?"

"We saw him," Salome said excitedly. "No one wants to believe us."

"Him? Of whom do you speak?" he meekly questioned.

Joanna drew even more near. "The Master. In the garden. Early this morn."

"You went to the tomb? Where were the guards? Do you know who took the body? I need to help find Him, secure His resting place. I..."

"They mean they saw *Him alive*, Centurion," exclaimed Sam. "*Risen, as He said he would.*"

"Yes. Yes," Mary added excitedly. "Those very words! A heavenly man sat there, seated on the slab of stone where the Master's body lay. He used those very words. How, kind sir, did you know?" she asked, turning to Sam. "Did you see him too?"

"This is Samuel Antonius...from Rome." Cornelius spoke in clipped sentences, still astonished, it seemed, by the favorable turn of events. "He has been with me...with me the entire night and day. I found him at the inn with Cleopas in Emmaus. What you said, though.... I am confused by it. You are not speaking of Jesus. Surely he cannot be alive!"

"Why, yes. The Master, Jesus!" Mary cried, the delight in her voice rising with each joy-filled phrase. "He has risen! We saw him with our own eyes. At the garden tomb. The stone was rolled back, the guards had vanished. Two beings in glorious white apparel spoke to us. 'He is not here,' they said, 'but risen as he said he would.' Then we saw!"

"No..." Cornelius gasped. "I heard a voice, but thought it imagination, the kind when..."

"What?" Joanna begged. "You heard what?" she interrupted.

His voice stopped me from killing the Tribune, he marveled to himself. *I was going to make him pay for his crimes.* "His voice from..." he rushed out the open door and squinted towards the end of the alley. "Surely, it is my mind playing tricks on me...."

Sam was witnessing an extension of the drama, an additional gap in narrative so emotion-packed, yet never recorded in the Gospels. He recalled now, though faintly, that the scriptures spoke of a number of faithful women having stood by at the crucifixion. And it had been several women, including Mary, wife of Cleopas, who had come with the other Mary and the mother of Jesus that morning to the empty tomb. "My God!" he mouthed under his breath.

Cornelius, hearing Sam's barely audible words, called to him. "Hurry. Make haste. Let us go to Cleopas and the others. Samuel, come!" He waved his companion out of the small city dwelling and into the alleyway. "The streets are not yet safe, Mary. You women stay," he gently commanded. "I will send for you this eve with my soldiers as escort. If, by chance, I do not come, do not move from here until I do arrive. I will notify Cleopas and whomever else I find at the home of John Mark's family. You mustn't share this news with anyone until we understand what is happening."

A sense of urgency propelled Sam to pose a question. The rarest of opportunities a true skeptic could imagine had presented itself. He directed his query to the women, asking, "Before we go, may I ask you this... Are you certain that you saw this Jesus of Nazareth alive this day, and not some look alike?"

All three women responded as one, with a mixture of testifying tears and vigorous nods of the head. "We saw...Him! All three of us saw," Salome answered with a catch in her voice.

"I saw," Mary added. "I know my Master well. It was He."

"I too beheld his presence," Joanna said.

"This was not some spirit, a ghost, a vision?" Sam asked.

Cornelius paid careful attention to Sam's interrogatories.

"He looked real. Mary of Magdala, as well, saw him, separate from us. And Mary his mother saw what we saw. A mother surely knows her own son! How could it be anything but what He said, that He would rise from the dead on the third day?" Mary of Emmaus, Cleopas' wife, gently assured.

"Samuel," Cornelius interrupted. "We must hurry. My services are needed. The followers' lives are in danger. If this gets out to Caiaphas, that these women saw Him, or believe they did, then no one is safe. We must hurry. Come."

"You saw?" Sam asked once more.

Mary approached him and in a voice unfailing and calm said, "Samuel Antonius, I swear to you this: I saw my Master, Jesus of Nazareth, alive. Now go tell my husband Cleopas."

Sam gazed into her eyes for any trace of deception. He thought of Rachel's eyes. These were like hers. He had always been able to read eyes. In these he found the sure knowledge that only the pure in heart know. She believed what she said.

Cornelius called from the door. "Samuel! It is time for you to report. Let us hurry! Come!"

26

THE DISCIPLES

Cleopas was a man overwhelmed by sorrow. The Master's body had been taken; his wife was missing; the disciples were just gathering. A rumor was circulating, the fantastic tale of several women - perhaps one being his own wife - had reported seeing Jesus alive. Upon hearing the report, Peter and John had rushed to the tomb. John, full of love and anxiety, together with the despairing Peter now mingled with hope, were not expected back at least until they could meet with the women of Bethany.

Cleopas was now at the home of John Mark, doing what he did best: preparing a meal for the followers who might arrive. He wanted to do something, anything, to help comfort his friends and brethren. But all this talk of resurrection, a preposterous, fantastic idea, likely the unreal expectations of the youthful and beloved John and John Mark, who was even now at the marketplace purchasing victuals...

The innkeeper wagged his weary head. He should have gone directly to Bethany the night previous, been there with his wife. It was late, however, and too dangerous for any even remotely accused of association with Jesus' "rebellion," as the high priest had called it, to be out in public.

Pacing the floor now, he answered a knock at the door. "Matthew, have you heard?"

"Shalom, Cleopas. I have heard. Even if it were true, I was a coward. I ran. I suppose the rest of the brethren are here?" he asked hopefully.

"You are the first."

"Oh. May I rest?"

"Of course. Please," he motioned. "Pillows," he said, pointing to one corner. "I am preparing supper. Soon we expect to hear from John and Peter. They went to the tomb."

"I passed by the house of Martha. She told me what the women saw. She said that your Mary was there."

"Is she there? My Mary? Is she safe?" an anxious Cleopas questioned.

"I did not see her. Someone said she had gone into Jerusalem, not far from here. The home of Salome and Joanna."

Cleopas dashed up the stairs to the upper window. Through partially closed shutters he peered out, knowing his beloved might be just streets apart from him. He deliberated in self-talk, partly to calm his nerves. *Should I go to her? I promised to wait for Cornelius.*

Matthew slumped back onto a pillow, put his hands to his head. "I never thought he would die. Not really. I believed he was the Messiah, come to unshackle Israel from the bonds of Rome and the false King Herod. Restore the ancient glory. I never thought he would die. But this tale told by the women. Fantastic..." He reclined against the wall in ponderous silence, eyes closed.

Cleopas paced more, wondering, trying to fathom this notion of resurrection. It was an ancient teaching, and one sometimes alluded to by Jesus. But he had not understood it to mean that one who dies actually is restored to his body. No, that had be but a metaphor for living forever in one's glorified, perfected spirit body. *What if? What if He was the Son of God, truly?*

Knowing that more of the followers likely would be arriving soon to this place where they last dined with the Master, Cleopas hesitated to leave; yet, he wanted to go find his Mary. He had also promised his child Sariah he would return to the inn this eve in Emmaus. Still, he stayed put. This would be the place they would congregate, all of them to muse on the latest events, consider the next steps, examine via interview these reports from the women.

"It is true!" John Mark called as he rushed up the steps from the tiny courtyard below. "He is not in the tomb!" he cried, his face fairly beaming. "He is risen!"

A knock came from below.

"Romans? Temple guard perhaps come to arrest us?" Matthew ventured, awakened now from his reverie.

"I will go see," John Mark offered. "He is risen as He said He would," the young man added with glee.

"Careful, lad," Cleopas urged.

A quiet moment lapsed. Cleopas stationed himself just inside the upper door, meat cleaver in hand, willing to defend Matthew, if necessary. Whisperings issued from below. Seeming to recognize the voices, he relaxed his grip.

"Romans, indeed," reported John Mark, smiling as he entered. Behind him loomed the massive frame of Centurion Cornelius and Samuel Antonius.

"Friend!" Cleopas cried. "And Samuel?" he said, dropping the jagged kitchen utensil.

Sam nodded and stood aside to take in this long-anticipated reunion. He patted his chest and arms with his hands. Strangely solid. Again he wondered how long this night of dreams would last.

Cornelius greeted his fellow believer. "I am glad to see you, Cleopas. I bring news. Your wife is with Joanna and Salome. We just came from the place where they reside. They are safe. I instructed them to be still and remain there until this day passes."

"Well, then. Thank you, Centurion!" said Cleopas, taking the other's hand in a firm grip of brotherhood. "I knew I could count on you! Ever our friend."

"The women may have saved us. Some treachery and maneuver by Tribune Valerius and his guards blindsided Samuel and I as we passed this way. Fortuitous it was that precisely where the women were, Samuel could take refuge whilst I troubled with Valerius."

"Did you kill him?" posed an eager John Mark.

"No, and you mustn't wish it, although I admit that in self-defense it might have been the case," he said, adding, "A voice stopped me as I readied to dispatch the devil."

"A voice?" Cleopas questioned. "Who's voice?"

"I cannot be sure. But it was familiar, and he called me by name as he stood at the end of the street. He also called me servant and *friend*. I was suddenly disarmed."

"By Valerius?" John Mark asked.

"No, by the voice. I let Valerius depart in peace. He knows he was beaten. He will not try anything further for a long while. His pride must recover first. But the voice...his words..." Cornelius's ruminations trailed off and the room went still in anticipation.

Finally Cleopas piped up. "And news? You said you bring news? Did it have to do with this voice?"

Matthew yet lounged in the corner. Silent, only now did he stir, sitting upright to listen.

"News of Pilate?" John Mark interjected. "Will they come after us?" He appeared excited at the prospect, as if eager for the plot to thicken.

"Pilate wishes nothing more than all of this to go away. It is the High Priest and his fellows who stir the pot of trouble. They claim the followers have stolen the body and bribed the guards. Pilate believes they did, so for now the matter is at an impasse. I believe all will be quiet for several days, each party hoping to make the other stumble, each sending out spies." The Centurion's mind drifted to another topic, and he turned to face Sam, saying nothing; pensive, as if a sudden thought occurring to him had wrought another puzzle piece and caused it to fit where it should.

"And my wife? She will not accompany us to Emmaus?" posed Cleopas.

"No, she will stay. I am sorry, Cleopas. But I took it upon myself. It is better. We should leave soon."

"And Samuel? You have not stayed with the Procurator and your fellows. I do not understand."

"Nor do I," replied the librarian-reporter. "So this is the place. The last supper was here?" his tone, one of reverence.

All stopped and turned to him, questioning him with their eyes. *How would he know?* Even Cornelius had not mentioned it, nor was he sure of it.

"Who are you, sir?" implored a voice from the corner. "And what do you know of the last Passover between us? If you be friend, make yourself known."

"Matthew, this is a gentleman who happened upon my inn," explained Cleopas. "He knows our story. I assure you that with Cornelius here, we have no need to fear. Samuel, too, is considered our friend."

"So be it. And welcome to you both." Matthew turned his attention on the Centurion, who had sprawled on several pillow near the center of the room. "Though this be a day mixed with disappointment and hope, I am glad to see you well. But why do we delude ourselves?" he sullenly offered from his dim-lit seat.

Sam, his confidence rising, spoke up. "You may be surprised to know that many outside of the promised land of Israel believe in life after death," he stated, part in earnest and part to provoke further comment, "...and that your cause is just."

Matthew arose and ambled across the room to size Sam up. Cornelius was quiet. Cleopas brooding and pacing once more, while John Mark, ever the admirer and observer, was at the ready to learn - even in this dark hour - from his elders when they counseled together.

"You believe as we do, then?" Matthew asked. "That Jesus of Nazareth was the Son of God? A Messiah sent to redeem Israel?"

"I know there are many believers, and the more I see and hear, the more sure I become. But as to faith, I am accustomed to seeing to believe," he answered.

His friend the innkeeper addressed him then. "Samuel. It is not a matter of the mind, but of the heart. This is faith, which stems from hope. You must learn this if you are to report to your people."

"So it is. In truth, it is so," Cornelius muttered in agreement.

Matthew, judging that Sam had spoken sincerely, let go of his doubts. "James should be here soon. Thomas? No one knows to where he fled. Philip and Andrew have gone to the fields where families gathered in camps for their return journey to the Galilee. They promised to come here directly after. As for the rest, I know not. Is our faith broken? Will Jesus return in spirit, as the women said He would?"

"They reported seeing his body, His physical body," said Sam, "saying that he was risen from death. Death and a real body cannot coexist. Perhaps your Master is risen?" Ever the prodding interviewer, he was tempting more words from them.

"Ah, if only..." Cleopas sighed. "I must make myself useful. John Mark, please assist me. We shall boil fish and prepare the condiments, then I shall depart with our friend, Centurion Cornelius, for Emmaus."

"Samuel will join us," Cornelius interjected. "I have been given charge to deliver him safely to the coast and straightway see him on a ship safely back to Rome. We must leave soon. It is mid-day and the city will be still. Perfect for our quiet departure."

Cleopas nodded and made eye contact with Matthew, who waved him to his chores. "I will not be long."

Sam smiled and shrugged, knowing he had no choice but to continue on... *At least until the anesthetics wear off,* he thought.

27

ROAD TO EMMAUS

And behold, two of them went that same day to a village called Emmaus, which was from Jerusalem about three-score furlongs. And they talked together of all these things which had happened.

-Gospel of Luke 24:13-14

No one had yet spoken. Sam trailed his two burly companions along the dusty road to Emmaus. The mood had been solemn and eerily peaceful - until now. Now safely away from the precincts of Jerusalem, the two disciples, Cleopas, Innkeeper of Emmaus, and Centurion Cornelius, talked quietly between themselves. Sam, keeping a respectful distance to the rear, was now the observer, as if watching a movie or play, detailed in every way but in the third person, without his presence in it.

He was beginning to realize that perhaps this was it, the price he must pay. He had feared it, had thought of it all night. He *was* dead, a fact he had been unwilling to believe until now. He had died from a broken heart, after all, a heart in part broken by years of abuse. The excesses and hopelessness of his life had killed him. He had never really attached any meaning to Rachel's appeals to become "whole," as she put it. And now he was sensing that this dream was about to end. *But to what end? What would come next?*

Is this my penance? He reflected. *Do I get to go to heaven? Hell? Without Rachel it might as well be,* he moodily concluded as he kept pace with the men on the road.

It seemed that they didn't even notice him now. It was as if he never existed to them. If he were dead, would this surreal movie - in which he was a main character - end and another begin? Perhaps he was condemned to live through multiple lifetimes past in order to learn lessons he should have learned during his mortality.

His deepest reflections and most earnest desires were for one more chance to see her eyes, her smile, taste her kiss, feel her warm body nestled comfortably up against his. Now if he had even a moment of that it would seem an undeserving but very welcome reward for enduring this video-like version of stories he had known with characters he had often read about while alive, but had never really cared to know.

Strange. He really liked these people. He really cared about them. He valued their simplicity, their faith, their pronounced child-like sorrow over the fate of their super-natural leader, Jesus. He suddenly was aware of their sacrifices, their determination, their innate goodness.

No, it was more like godliness, he thought. *Imitators of one they loved and believed in.* He even was feeling close to...

No! He had never proved anything but the contrary. He'd run from God his entire life, had always known in his heart of hearts that there must be one, a God out there, that the Christ story with its enduring appeal and power to convert must have something behind it...something greater than just nice words about love and brotherly kindness. But God was a long ways away, and *not at all convenient* to believe in. For him to have drawn near to this Jesus, he would have had to give up a lot of little pleasures, habits – *and* go to church. *Rachel would have been worth that,* he thought.

God be with you till we meet again, the line from the church hymn came. It struck him, out of the blue. Suddenly. He'd heard that line over and over at the end of meetings attended as a child, meetings his mother had insisted he attend. Rachel had even sung it to him, in practice for a solo she sang at a funeral just last week. *Such a good person,* he recalled with pride. *So giving,* he added in soliloquy.

Funeral... Maybe she will sing it at mine! The thought struck him with a panic he had not thought himself to possess. The pragmatic Sam had always managed to push fears away, as he had pushed God away. Even throughout this night of dreams, of madness, he had kept his stage presence, a sense of utter control.

Fears are not convenient. They made you think of unpleasant things. They made you contemplate things that belong to the dead and the damned, he once told a guest on his show.

Last week, in fact! To Cardinal McIntyre! He had uttered those exact words when the Cardinal had reminded him of what Jesus had said to his disciples: *Peace I leave with you... Peace and fear cannot exist at the same moment. I prefer peace. Don't you, Samuel?"* He had even called him Samuel, something no other guest had ever done!

Sam had blown the Cardinal off. Thanked him, but pushed his kind words away. He had Rachel. What better peace was there?

That was then.

But *now*... He looked up to see if his dreamland companions were still near at hand. He was surprised to see a third walking with them, some fifty meters ahead. Eager to again take in their musings, he picked up the pace, jogging, almost, drawing near to take in what he could. Maybe there was something here, some thread of hope for him in this new apparition.

He approached and veered to the right side of his fellows, off the narrow dirt road on the shoulder, nearest Cornelius, who had shed his military gear for the robes of a Judean. He strode along in pace with him now. Cornelius didn't look up nor over to see Sam. Rather, he was deeply pensive, eyes fixed upon the worn path at his feet, seeming to be looking for some answers there.

Sandwiched between Cleopas and Cornelius was the other man, similar in height, slighter in build than the burly Roman, clear complexioned and well-groomed from his beard to his shoulder-length locks of hair. Donning a head covering, his facial features were not distinguishable to Sam, but he spoke mildly and with earnest appreciation for the sorrow and confusion Cleopas and Cornelius shared with him.

"What is your name, friend?" asked the man, laying a hand lightly upon the Centurion's shoulder. Cornelius didn't flinch. Ever the proper soldier, trained to stand apart, aloof, this reaction was very unlike that of a Roman officer of the Legion. To feel the touch of a fellow traveler upon his arm or shoulder would be unthinkable. Yet, Cornelius calmly remained within this stranger's touch.

"I am known as Centurion Cornelius. I have shed my military dress this day to accompany my friend Cleopas to his inn. I was born Simon Lazaro, in the center of Iberia. Simon Cornelius is my Roman name, given by the family who adopted me as an orphaned child. Today I feel like that first Simon, a child, more than any day I can recall."

"You are sad," said the stranger.

"And I am confused. He healed my servant, and..." Cornelius frowned, unsure of this melancholy and why he should open his innermost thoughts and feelings to a stranger.

"And you, my friend?" the stranger turned, leaving Cornelius deep in his own thoughts. "Where do you venture and what name are you known by?"

"I am Cleopas, an innkeeper of Emmaus, son of Jacob but raised by my uncle Simeon in Bethlehem. Trained by him to be an innkeeper there, but that was long ago, and a sorry tale, too."

They walked a few paces more in silence. "Your hearts are much burdened. What is it that has you both so distressed?" the attentive stranger asked.

Sam stopped. His heart seemed to leap to the question. He recalled it all in an instant. He stood and watched as they moved on, then once more fell close behind them, not listening now but struggling to remember something from very long ago.

His mother had insisted on reading aloud the Bible at the dinner table each night, until she passed away in his thirteenth year. That was a bitter time. He never quite forgave God for taking her.

His mind was suddenly caught up in the story he had known since childhood. It was his mother's favorite, a tale she read and re-read perhaps two or three times each year. Certainly it was read at Christmastime, along with how the Innkeeper of Bethlehem turned the holy family away; then it was repeated again during the celebration of Easter week.

Sure. Makes sense now, he muttered to himself.

He was trudging along, putting one foot in front of another, but oddly lost in time and memory. He could see her now, see her plainly and hearing her words. It was the early '50s. It had been years since he had visualized the image of his overworked but soft-spoken, middle-aged mother. At the dinner table, just the two of them, they sat, dessert put on hold until the nightly ritual was completed.

Mother, he mouthed sincerely, involuntarily.

He could see the crisp, printed sentences lining the crinkly, finger-worn pages of the thick family Bible, saw them as if they were clearly set before him now! The onionskin sheet of this particular story so thoroughly read and marked with blue ink pen markings, showing where she felt special attention was needed, came back to him. They were here, on this road, in this dream, lying open before his eyes.

Each word, each sentence came to him now, her voice quietly ringing in his inner ears. He'd lost sight of the three men and the road he trod, even though he knew his travel companions were still nearby and the dirt road was yet underfoot. His only thoughts were of her and the verses she so loved.

"Mother," he whispered again with a smile. "Is that you?" He closed his eyes and trusted his feet to carry him from this place, following these three ancient men, to wherever the overseer of this trance intended for it to wend.

"Samuel," she sweetly reminded. "It is your turn to read. And remember, it is not always what you *see* that matters, but what you *feel*. You can know things in your heart that your mind cannot be certain of. *Trust your heart*, Samuel. Now, read to me my favorite story, the story of two who needed to learn that very lesson."

He was a child, curled up next to her on the sofa. The fire was aglow, its embers dancing softly behind the lattice metal screen below the mantelpiece. This time the dessert had already been eaten. He watched his mother close her eyes as she waited for the boy to read to her from the final chapter of Luke:

And it came to pass, that, while they communed together and reasoned, Jesus himself drew near, and went with them. But their eyes were holden that they should not know him.

And he said unto them, What manner of communications are these that ye have one to another, as ye walk, and are sad?

And one of them, whose name was Cleopas, answering said unto him, Art thou only a stranger in Jerusalem, and hast not known the things which are come to pass there in these days?

And he said unto them, What things? And they said unto him, Concerning Jesus of Nazareth, which was a prophet mighty in deed and word before God and all the people:

And how the chief priests and our rulers delivered him to be condemned to death, and have crucified him. But we trusted that it had been he which should have redeemed Israel: and beside all this, today is the third day since these things were done. Yea, and certain women also of our company made us astonished, which were early at the sepulcher;

And when they found not his body, they came, saying, that they had also seen a vision of angels, which said that he was alive—and certain of them which were with us went to the sepulchre, and found it even so as the women had said: but him they saw not.

Then he said unto them, O fools, and slow of heart to believe all that the prophets have spoken:

Ought not Christ to have suffered these things, and to enter into his glory? And beginning at Moses and all the prophets, he expounded unto them in all the scriptures the things concerning himself.

And they drew nigh unto the village, whither they went: and he made as though he would have gone further.

But they constrained him, saying, Abide with us: for it is toward evening, and the day is far spent. And he went in to tarry with them.

"Mother?" Sam said the word aloud as he came to himself in the sudden realization that he had been day-dreaming – a dream within a dream. He looked up in time to see the three men entering the inn; they had reached Emmaus! He had followed behind, barely noticing one step after the other. *Slow of heart to believe,* he thought.

"Hey, Cleopas! Wait!" he shouted after them. "Hey! I'm still here! Cornelius!"

Hurrying to the doorway into which the three had disappeared, he peeked in. The men were alone in the room, seated cross-legged at a table that rose no higher than one foot off the floor. The stranger sat between his two friends. Pillows were scattered about the room, left by guests now departed for their homes afar off. Sam stepped inside and ventured closer, until he stood in the shadows of the curtain separating the dining hall from the serving area. *Strange,* he thought. *All night, perhaps for days, I am companion to these two men in a surgically sedated illusion, and now it is as if I don't even exist.*

Now something new did take hold of him, causing him to wonder where the veil of reality parted when one entered a never-land so full of mind concocted imagery; characters and life as this. It was a deep, deep sensation in his very center that whispered: *This is as it was.*

Sam felt the inner stirrings of childhood once more. The believer in whatever his mother said was a part of him now. She would never lie; not her. He whispered her name in sacred remembrance. *Gloria Robertson... This very event you taught me to believe deeply; right here,* he said to himself as he held one hand over his heart. "*I do believe. I do, Mother. I do believe it, Mother...*" he repeated softly, over and over again.

And it came to pass, as he sat at meat with them, he took bread, and blessed it, and brake, and gave to them. And their eyes were opened, and they knew him; and he vanished out of their sight.

And they said one to another, Did not our heart burn within us, while he talked with us by the way, and while he opened to us the scriptures?

Sam fell to his knees. He had not felt such emotions in a very long time, did not understand really what had overcome him. The stranger brushed by him now. He seemed to stop, glance down at Sam. Sam immediately looked away, whether out of shame, fear...he wasn't sure, but he could not look the man in the face, could not see the stranger clearly if he tried. It wasn't the dimness of the room, but the overflowing moisture stinging his eyes.

He felt a mild voice call to him within. *"Samuel..."*

Was the man still there? Though he wished to, he could not lift his head; he could not face this man. Why was he crying like a child? What had overcome him? His heart was broken, needed repair. All he wanted to do was go back home. This man could do that for him. He sensed it within.

"Samuel," the voice again called to his innermost soul. *"Be ye whole."*

"I know you," he whispered. *"She believed,"* he cried unashamedly. *"Mother did and... and..."* he sobbed, collapsing upon the ground. Lost and out of control, he wanted - but couldn't - bring the proper words to the surface.

"Rachel- She tried to tell me, explain it to me. See, my mind would not let me believe until I could see. I required visual proof and... I... uh...," he finally said, but could not finish expressing his innermost thoughts, could not get past the pent up years of cynicism stored in a file of emotions deep within the mind.

His heart took over; felt the flame now. It wasn't a raging inferno, but rather like the warmth of peaceful embers from a fireplace in boyhood years past - and it seemed to gently melt away at the cold center of his chest. With one hand over his heart, he reached down with the other to raise himself to his knees. The sensation washing over him swept from the bottom of his feet up into his very center, then to his head and back like a warm light. He surged with energy, a tonic the doctors, with all their good intentions, could never prescribe. Like loving Rachel, this was a euphoria unearned, undeserved. Like loving Rachel, it filled him with inexplicable joy.

"*I'm free!*" he exclaimed giddily. "*I'm well!*"

Bowing his head in gratitude, he dared not believe the dream, dared not accept this healing of his soul, and his heart. Now, the blessed apparition was leaving him. Kneeling upon the hard floor of the inn, he reached out in hopes of touching the stranger as he passed by. The words escaped from deep within Sam, in gasps of childlike hope and grateful tears...

28

RACHEL IS THAT YOU?

"Oh Lord, my God," he cried. "Oh Lord, my God," he tearfully pled, reaching up in supplication for forgiveness and understanding.

"Mr. Robertson," the nurse's gentle voice called to him as he clutched her hand. "Mr. Robertson!" she repeated, this time more insistently. "You are not supposed to be out of bed! Someone call the doctor on duty," she shouted to the nursing station outside the door of the room.

Sam was doubled over on the cold tile floor of New York City Hospital's intensive care ward. It was late into the evening. He was still partially hooked up to the monitors, but not responding to the nurse's pleas.

"Mr. Robertson? This is Nurse Watkins." She knelt down next to him, tried to move him, but he wouldn't let go of her hand. "Mr. Robertson, please! Wake up now. Let me help you back into bed."

"Oh, my!" a nurse gasped from the doorway. Several more came running, with Doctor Peterson and the on-call physician close behind.

Uniting as a team, they helped lift Sam back into the bed. "Why is he crying? What's happened here?" asked Doctor Peterson.

The nurse, a bit rattled, tried to explain. "I came in and found Mr. Robertson on the floor. He was crying. He grabbed my hand and wouldn't let go - just kept praying. I have no idea why the rail was down or how he fell out..."

"Well, let's take a look," Peterson said. "This man was near death last time I looked in on him, and now..."

The on-call physician, Doctor Stockwell, leaned over Sam, then turned to the head nurse. "Call cardiology. See if you can raise Doctor Gray. If you can't, try for Whitaker."

Nurse Watkins took a brief look at the chart and rushed off for the nursing station. Both doctors now took to examining Sam from either side of the bed, when Rachel appeared at the door.

"What's going on?" she asked the nearest nurse, a nervous catch in her voice.

The nurse smiled and patted her on the arm. "He'd gotten himself out of bed and was having some sort of nightmare. Let's give the doctors a few minutes, then they'll catch you up on everything. Okay?" She turned Rachel away from the scene and suggested they go to the ICU waiting room.

"I want to stay," Rachel insisted.

"Rachel?" Sam called weakly. "Rachel? Is that you?"

29

MIRACLE

48 Hours Later

"Amazing, I must say, Rachel!" Doctor Peterson exclaimed. "His heart rate, the blood work, the tests we've done, all indicate his heart is on the mend. For a man who was near death, touch and go, this is a much healthier looking heart." He tapped the file folder set in front of him, containing the x-rays they'd taken over two days before. "We need to watch him this week and, if this keeps up, he'll be heading home for Christmas."

Down the hall, Doctor Gray shook his head and probed once more with his stethoscope. "Congratulations, Mr. Robertson. It's remarkable; truly amazing. I don't recall any recovery like it, especially of a man your age, the condition of your heart in full cardiac arrest... Well, they reserve the term 'miracle' for these occasions. Something or someone besides this staff pulled you through. I'd like to take the credit, but, frankly, I wouldn't have been surprised to see you with a bed sheet over your head at my next visit."

Sam blew out a sigh. "It took prayers," he said simply, he voice weak yet steady. He reached up to take the doctor's outstretched hand. "No doubt about it, Doc. I'm really grateful to you, to all of you."

"Well, I'll see you this evening. At this rate, I'll be seeing you on nightly television again, too."

Minutes later, Rachel appeared at the door. Sam smiled, waved her in, and searched her eyes. "I thought I'd never see you again," he whispered.

She stroked his hair, kissed his forehead. "I was worried about that too."

"So you were praying, huh?"

She slid a chair up to his bead and reached for his hands. "A lot of people were praying. Cards, letters, e-mails, too many to count, from people all over the country. Messages from friends have poured in, all the people in the business, they've been sending their well-wishes and prayers. People love you, Sam. I knew they did, but I had no idea how many you'd touched."

"I haven't touched anyone. Not really," he replied quietly, earnestly. "I'm a different man. In here," he said, patting his chest. "Remember that night at the restaurant? Right before..." He stopped. Glassy eyed, he tried to say what he was feeling, but found that the words wouldn't come out.

"Oh, Sam," she whispered. "I remember. I was so hard on you. I felt so bad. I just wanted you to have something... I thought... See, I felt you were missing out, and..." Rachel, too, began to stumble over the myriad emotions pouring out of her, unable to connect the hodgepodge of words to describe the way she felt about him.

Sam gently squeezed her hands. "It's alright now. Everything's all right. I've been somewhere only this heart disease could have taken me. I have a lot to tell you. But I want you to know something."

He smiled, reached up to brush her silky auburn hair with his fingertips. He placed his hand on her arm, then over her heart. "Here. Right here. Now I understand, baby. I understand in a way I can't totally describe. I understand what you were trying to say before. I know who sent you back, gave you life again when you were a scared little girl at St. Jude's Hospital. I understand the words now. What they meant."

She laid her head on his chest and listened to the steady, rhythmic beating of his heart. "A big heart, Sam," she said through the tears.

"And, Rachel, honey," he softly whispered. "I'm finally *whole*."

30

ROBERTSON CHRISTMAS SHOW

<u>Upper West Side Manhattan</u>

"Sam, do you really think this is a good idea? Everyone will understand. Your producer said they already have the 'best of' *Sam Robertson Reports - The Christmas Shows* ready to play all week. Why don't you put this off. Give it one more week. Stay home...relax."

Rachel leaned past the door, fluttering her big "Bambi eyes," putting on the pout he adored. He saw through her playfulness, to the genuine concern she was trying to mask. She was trying to dissuade him from going through with this. She had taken his overcoat hostage, hiding it behind her back.

"Rachel, I have a story to tell," he said, gesturing for the coat. "It's Christmas Eve. I'm a 'miracle man,' remember? Doctor Gray even wrote it on my chart. You wouldn't want me to keep the gratitude I owe to all those who prayed for me locked up here with us over the holidays, would you?"

"Sam...you know I don't. I just worry, that's all."

"You'll be right there with me, right? What can go wrong?"

She frowned, then shook her head. "Here," she said, holding out the coat. "But I'm keeping my eye on you."

"I wouldn't want it any other way." He smiled, put on the coat, kissed her, and helped her on with her coat. "I love you. Let's go tell the world."

Their driver, Tony, was waiting as they exited the building. "Mr. Robertson. I hope you don't mind. Here's a Christmas card and a package for you." He waved an envelope and smiled. "People all day saying how glad they are that you're back at it."

"Thanks, Tony," Sam replied. "Who's it from? You can't be too careful nowadays." He bent towards the driver's ear as Rachel scooted across the backseat. "Could be a letter bomb," he whispered.

Tony laughed off the comment, but brandished the envelope in a way that told Sam he wasn't entirely convinced the note was harmless. "I'm sorry. Really, Mr. Robertson, I didn't think... Guess I should'a had security check it out," he said, checking his mirrors. "The man, he was so nice. Big fella; looked Italian, ya' know. He's new with the company, I think. Said he'd been a deliveryman for years. Said he was gonna' take my place this afternoon so I can hit my family's Christmas Eve party."

He looked around the busy sidewalk, hoping to see the man. "Hmm. Where'd he go? He was just here a minute ago; dropped off the package. Anyway," he said, pulling out into traffic, "you know us paisanos — we look out for each other."

Sam opened the envelope and took out the folded card inside. It read: "Welcome home, Samuel. See you at Farouk's after the show. Signed: An old friend."

An old friend. Sam's mind began to wander. *Probably one of my pals from the radio show days back in the '70s,* he thought. *Gave it to the stand-in driver who handed it over to Tony....*

Tony returned to his jargon-filled patter. "This other guy, he's gotta' take over for me. Probably'll be more careful with ya' - you know, guard you against letter bombs and everything." Tony grinned, then scratched his head and glanced out onto the throng of holiday shoppers crossing the intersection ahead. "Maybe he went for coffee," he mused, revisiting for yet a third time the new guy who'd be subbing for him that evening.

"Tony, the card says, 'See you at Farouk's after the show.' But there's no package here."

"Hey, no sweat then, Mr. 'R.' Maybe the guy kept it to give you tonight at Farouk's. Like I said, I hope you don't mind, but I got this party, family and all, ya' know. And the new guy there in the office volunteered to bring you back from the studios. Course, if ya' want, I can call home and cancel, tell them to start the party without me."

Sam chuckled at the driver's sincerity, his considerate offer. It was the same sort of caring and kindness he'd received for the three weeks since his release from the hospital.

"No, Tony. You celebrate the birth of the Christ child. Enjoy your family. But, if you can, I'd be honored to know that you tuned in to my Christmas message tonight."

"Hey, you got it, Mr. Robertson. I'll just gather the family around the TV to hear your story. We'll make it part of the celebration, finding out how you came back from the dead and all."

Sam lifted an eyebrow. He slid a few inches closer to Rachel and smiled over at her, thinking, *You sure got that one right, Tony. You surely did!*

31

THE CHRIST REPORT

"It's a miracle. Don't know what vitamins you've been taking, but for all practical purposes you've got the heart of a forty year-old," Sam said, recounting Doc Peterson's words as he mingled with his radio show crew at the party. Platters filled with Christmas delicacies were strewn about the ribbon and tree ornament-trimmed table. "Then he said," Sam continued, "'I've never seen such a reversal in all my years of practice.' And with that, Doc Peterson walked out. That was yesterday. I've got to tell you, though, it wasn't any special vitamins or diet or anything like that."

Sam and Rachel had arrived two hours early to set out their Christmas gifts and greet the CNTV staff and crew he'd worked with for so many years now. Each had expressed in turn their heartfelt words of support for Sam. And then it was his producer Mary Kelly's turn. "Sam Robertson, you leave me no choice," she began, an odd seriousness in her words. "You're fired!" Then, through a wide smile set beneath tear-stained cheeks, she threw her arms around him and exclaimed, "I'm going to miss you so much."

He drew her close, gave a peck on the cheek and then looked her in the eye. "Mary? You can cry! I'm touched."

"Oh, shut up," she whimpered, giving him a light slap on the shoulder, "or I'll find some way to keep you in your contract!" Then she handed him an envelope with her Christmas greeting. "I've decided this is it for me, too. I'm retiring...."

"No! Really? Rachel, did you hear that?"

Rachel was at his side. "What made you decide. Is this for real?"

Mary wiped her face and took a few moments to regain her composure. "Sam's life nearly ending, then his second chance," she croaked in a voice barely above a whisper. "It got me to thinking how this place has been my life, my religion, too. Seven days a week, my mind's always here. Now my kids are grown and I've got a couple of grandchildren I hardly ever see. I don't need the money. Without Sam, there's just not much point in me staying on."

Sam pulled her close again. "Mary, I think you've made an excellent decision. You deserve it. And Frank, he deserves it, too. He's a lucky guy. I'm going to call him right after the show and congratulate him for getting you back."

"Right here, Sam. I owe you," came a voice from behind Sam.

He spun around. "Frank, good to see you here. How'd you sneak in?"

"Just waited my turn. Quite a long reception line, you know," he said smiling. They embraced like brothers.

"Don't let her get away from you again, Frank. Make her happy to be home. Travel, enjoy the kids and grandkids. I can tell you, almost losing Rachel, thinking I wasn't going to make it, it all put things into perspective."

"We thought a lot about it, and about you, Sam. The world isn't going to be the same without your mug on TV and that bowtie starring at us each night. You can't be replaced."

"How sweet, Frank," Rachel offered.

"Sam Robertson Reports *live*. I kinda' like the sound of that," Frank replied. "Well, we better get to the stage. Take care," he said with a wave.

Sam turned to Rachel. "Be there for me, baby. As long as I know you're there, I can get through this."

"I'll be sitting right off the side of camera 1. You can count on it. And then I'm taking you home for a Christmas Eve to remember."

Sam took her in his arms, held her close, kissed her forehead. "You are God's greatest gift to me." He winked, turned to head off to the stage, felt her fingers slip away from his. He made his way to his position behind the desk. The familiar city skyline backdrop, recognized by so many people worldwide, filled the TV monitor to his left. He drew in a deep breath and pondered on his final, career-ending message, what he now considered to be the report of his career. He had wrestled with what he should call it, this, his final show, and had decided in his heart of hearts that it would be known simply, and with a name appropriate to his dreamscape experience weeks ago. After all, it was in worldwide celebration of the nativity. If anyone was offended by its title, well, they could just switch channels. He needed to do what he needed to do.

He hadn't been able to explain to Rachel what he might say. For that matter, he didn't fully know himself what he was about to say.... Maybe it was fear he was feeling. Or maybe for him it was simply too sacred a message to tell more than once. He wanted to do this right, thank his Maker for another chance, for a new heart, for the newfound faith he had received, and for the blessing of being able to spend more time with his beloved wife; all gifts beyond price. So this was it. It would be something so out of character, as far as what the world knew him to be. He swallowed hard...took a sip of water...waited.

Straightening his tie and brushing a hand through his slightly graying head of hair, he looked on as Mary, fingers raised, counted down the last few seconds. Then, on cue, staring into camera 1, he began:

"Welcome to this Christmas Eve edition of *Sam Robertson Reports*. And you have no idea how happy it makes me to be able to say that! First, I want to extend to all you viewers my profound gratitude for your cards, letters and prayers that sustained Rachel and me through my most recent life-and-death ordeal."

He turned on cue to camera 2.

"Back from the brink, I thank our sponsors, friends, associates and supporters everywhere; you'll never know how deeply I feel about my life on and off the air with you. We have shared thousands of good times, reports from all over the world, events that have shaken the history of nations.

"A little over a month ago when my head hit the pillow in an operating room, I came close to never again speaking to you. It was during that long night of slumber, under the spell of anesthetics in a hospital ward with a heart beating at a snail's pace, that I found myself in the fight for my life.

"I desperately wanted to live, to have a second chance to be with my beautiful wife Rachel, to feel her love and stay even one more year here with her – and with you, my friends. That night-of-nights has changed me. I can no longer sit at this desk and do *Sam Robertson Reports*. This Christmas Eve is my final broadcast.

"And though I regret to say this will be my final report, I am confidant that what I offer is the report of a lifetime.

"My report is one of a dying man's search for faith and meaning as he attempts to hold on to life, and to the woman, the new love, he has found.

"Consider this: If a reporter were to be given a last chance to interview someone before dying, who would it be, and what would he ask?

"This, a Christmas Eve broadcast, is my parting Christmas gift to you. I dreamt a vivid dream during the long night when my body lay in the cold grip of mortal struggle. The dreamy story I report to you was one I could not have conjured up in my wildest fantasies.

"I wandered away from the hospital, sometime between surgery and awakening in my recovery room. I found myself in an incredible time and place. I must say incredible because nothing like it exists today in the world, and I have traveled the world over many times.

"Although ethereal, I must say that those dreamland events, even now, seem as real as anything I ever experienced. This may sound crazy, but please indulge me. It's a Christmas story, after all.

"I dreamt I was taken back in time. The day was the first day after the man Jesus of Nazareth was nailed to the cross. The place, Jerusalem.

"There was one named Cleopas, an innkeeper from a village called Emmaus, and a Roman Centurion known simply by him as *the Friend*... Together, they took me on a path I never would have chosen to wander.

"I made a promise in my sleeping state which I intend now to keep. The promise? To make a report of my visit with them; to make amends for a man troubled by a mistake that must now, this Christmas, be rectified. I cannot live with myself unless I give an account of his story. So...at this season of gift-giving, I share with you a treasure some two thousand years in the making. I call this final broadcast, *THE CHRIST REPORT!*"

32

THE INNKEEPER'S GIFT

"Thank you," Rachel said to the smiling, broad-shouldered man who held the door to the limousine. "You're driving for Tony tonight?"

"Yes," he answered simply, then asked, "Mr. Robertson coming with us?"

"Oh, he asked me to have you pull around the back. He has some gifts from the studio he'd like to load into the trunk."

"Yes, ma'am." The driver pushed shut the back curbside passenger door and walked around the front of the long sedan to the driver's side. "Beautiful day. Christmas Eve always is, though," he said pleasantly, positioning himself behind the wheel. "And a fine chariot," he noted, patting the limo's padded steering wheel.

"What?" She giggled at his choice of words. She was still rehearsing in her mind the story as told by Sam an hour earlier, pondering the details of his dream-like visit to an era filled of both darkness and light. "Odd you should call it that. You were really involved in Sam's storytelling, I take it."

The big man chuckled. "You might say. I have an affinity for happy endings too. Congratulations on yours," he said, glancing into his rearview mirror. "Shall we?"

"Ready."

Rachel felt finally at peace. Sam had healed miraculously. He had been given a gift she knew was from God – whether others considered it miraculous or merely a fine Christmas tale. She actually knew it would have had to be something deeply moving to trigger in Sam such a radical change of heart. He was a thinker, after all, one not easily given to persuasion without hard evidence. Something happened during his coma-like state in that cardiac intensive care unit. Between death's door and new life, Sam knew something his heart now trusted, and his mind could simply tell it in story form.

"Here we are." The driver popped the trunk open and began to step out to help Sam load the packages.

"No need, my friend. Just stay put. We've got it," Sam called out. Several members of the crew, along with Mary and her husband, had helped transport the stack of gifts from Sam's CNTV studio family down the back stairs to the curb.

While Sam loaded the trunk, Rachel rolled her window down to say goodbye to Mary and give her a final kiss on the cheek. Then Sam scooted into the seat beside her and waved farewell to his friends. "Home James," he said, smiling.

Driver's and Sam's eyes met; Sam looking into the rear view mirror, and strong smiling eyes of cobalt beaming back at him from the front seat. "I knew James," he mouthed quietly.

For the briefest moment Sam's eyes questioned the driver with the thought, *Do I know you?* Then he turned his attention to his beloved Rachel.

"That was lovely, Sam," said Rachel, sighing and leaning back into the soft leather seat. "I was so taken — so touched . You could launch a second career in fiction-writing with that kind of material."

"It wasn't fiction, Rachel." Sam slid an arm around her shoulders and pulled her close. "To me, it actually happened. It was like I was really there. Strange, even sitting there in front the cameras, I could almost smell the stews and hearth-baked breads at the inn, feel the dust from the streets of Jerusalem on my skin, hear the sounds of travelers on the road. It was so, so very real!" He gazed out the window at the crowded streets, his mind wandering. "So real..." he whispered.

Rachel peered intently into his eyes, now fixed straight ahead but misted over with memory, sensing that he had an experience and undergone a transformation that only he could fully comprehend. But she, too, knew something about the power of such an experience. Her childhood illness and the kind man who had brought her back from the light...well, skeptics could believe what they wanted, but she knew better. *So, Sam came back from a light, as well,* she thought.

"Here we are," the driver said with a smile. He was at the curb with the door open. Sam was still lost in quiet thought. Rachel waited, knowing he was savoring a memory, a sacred memory.

"Oh!" he started, suddenly aware. "We're home."

Light snowflakes had begun falling, gilding the nearby tree limbs and walks with a crystalline sheen. Sam caught a brief glimpse of the driver before he reached back and pulled a hood over his head. "Welcome home, Samuel Robertson," he said. "And a Merry Christmas to you and Rachel," he added.

The deep, penetrating baritone of the new driver awakened something in Sam. He got out of the car and stepped around to the driver's side door to face the man head on. Sam's mind began accessing thousands of mental files, searching snapshots of people, places, events. Nothing. The man's features struck an immediate, potent chord of warmth, but... Before he reached the driver, Rachel called out.

"Sam, honey," Rachel called from the limo's open trunk, "the doorman's here to help us unload. Could you give us a hand?"

"Sure, sweetheart. Be right there," he answered, still trying to place the blue eyes and face of a man he had only just now met through the mirror. Fumbling for his wallet and fishing out his last hundred-dollar bill, Sam approached the driver's door, opened it and said, "And have a Merry..." he stopped with a questioning expression. The man had vanished. *Must be with Rachel by the trunk...*

Turning, he saw Rachel at their apartment's lobby door with an armload of gifts. "Hey, Rachel," he called. "Where's the driver?"

"Last I saw he was wishing us a Merry Christmas," she shouted back. "Better hurry before you're caught in a blizzard," she added before disappearing inside.

Must have headed across the street to the deli while I fumbled with my wallet, he thought. He crossed the lightly traveled residential street and entered Farouk's, which was nearly set to close.

"Merry Christmas, Mr. Sammy," greeted the Egyptian store owner from behind the meat counter. "I watched your show. Everybody is talking, Mr. Sammy," Farouk added. "I hardly remembered I was working. What a story, I tell you."

Farouk was owner of the only Middle Eastern/Greek-American/Italian deli Sam had ever heard of. It was the one place where a man with a yen for a falafel, a side of potato salad, a slice of greasy pizza with extra cheese and an artery-clogging portion of baklava for dessert, could indulge himself.

"I'm looking for someone. A big man, the driver of my car. He disappeared and I thought maybe he came in here."

"Big like a football player, blue eyes like a German, dark like Italian, and a deep happy voice?" Farouk answered.

"Yeah, that's him."

"Sure. He came in and asked me to give you a package. Said you would understand. It's right here." He wiped his hands on his apron and hung it on a hook in the corner.

Sam felt a bit apprehensive. There was a gnawing sensation in his gut that was both pleasant and impatient – the way one feels while waiting for a loved one to arrive for a visit, or, he supposed, how an expectant parent might feel just before the birth of a child. His mind continued to race seeking to arrive at some resolution of where he'd met the man, the limo driver.

"Here we go, Mr. Sammy. And Merry Christmas," Farouk said, handing him the nondescript, solid, oblong package wrapped in plain brown paper.

Sam took it and angled it toward the light so as to more easily make out the handwriting:

To Samuel Robertson, in gratitude for the report.

"Hum, well thanks again, and Merry Christmas, Farouk."

"I just close the door behind you," he said, following Sam to the front. "Merry Christmas, Mr. Sammy."

Sam stepped out into the fast-accumulating snow that crunched underfoot as he walked. He tucked the package under his arm, looked both ways and jogged back across the street. There was a new vigor in his step, one he hadn't known for years. It surged in him. He was happy and feeling right about life. In fact, he never could have imagined a better ending, nor a more satisfying report on which to end his career than the one he'd delivered today, Christmas Eve.

33

PEACE BE UNTO YOU

Reaching the lobby door, Sam glanced back at the empty car, certain the driver would show up soon, hoping to thank him properly and spread some holiday cheer.

Christmas tunes... He alternately whistled and hummed along with the music that wafted from under his neighbor's doors as he made his way down the hall to the elevator doors. *Should have stolen Larry King's moniker "ROBERTSON LIVE!"* he mused happily.

A tune had stayed with him all that day, seemingly playing over and over in his mind. It was the country singer's rendition leading into his final *Robertson Reports.* *"...Humm, humm, humm, the angel sings, Christ is born today; that man might live for evermore, because of Christmas Day."* He reached for his keys. *It should be illegal to be so happy,* he thought.

"In here," Rachel called from the corner near the tree. Two mugs of hot cocoa sat on the end table next to the couch. "Let's sit by the fireplace and relax. Now, forever, it's just you and me. Life is good, Sam," she said, smiling. "Come." She patted the seat next to her.

He hung up his overcoat, then brought the package over, kicked off his shoes, fell onto the cushioned sofa and propped his feet up on the hearth to let the glowing, gas-lit flames do their magic.

"What's that?" she asked, seeing the package.

"Don't know. I was looking for the driver, and went over to Farouk's to see if he'd gone in there. Guess he had, because he left this for me. Strange fellow. Could have handed it to me himself."

"Open it," she urged. "Go on. Let's make it the first."

"Oh...if you insist," he said with a grin that no one would be able to wipe from his face this day. He was *alive*! Every cell in his body vibrated with happiness, assuring him that life was not only good, but an extraordinary miracle. He slid his finger along one edge of the loose wrapping and tugged at the string that crisscrossed on the sides and tied into a bow on top. Rather rustic packaging, in fact. He kept up his soft whistling, humming, singing combination, marveling at his good fortune, the blessing of having Rachel next to him in this moment. It was the beginning of *their* time, an ongoing series of days and nights in which he would never have to be away from her again.

"Well?" she asked.

He paused as the rough paper was removed. His stare was locked on the parcel's contents, his gaze suddenly miles from Rachel, all in an instant.

"Sam, honey? Something wrong?"

His heart unexpectedly skipped a beat, then went into warp-speed. His hands trembled as he ran his fingers over the edge of the rectangular object sitting in his lap, still padded in lamb's fleece and tied with leather cords, which loosened effortlessly as his fingers fumbled with the knots.

He gently drew the musty fleece covering away to expose a carved wooden plank, one inch thick, about a foot in length and some eight inches wide.

Scorch marks! His eyes watered, his mind swimming against the current of the impossible. Momentarily paralyzed, lost in thought, he revisited the story in his mind, then leapt to his feet.

The writing engraved upon the wood... *The words!* He let them play in his mind over and over again. His fingers shook as they caressed the inscribed Hebrew lettering. *It can't be!* he breathed with reverence.

A piece of near-transparent onion skin paper that had been tucked beneath the board fell free and drifted to the floor. "Sam, sweetheart! What is it?" Rachel picked up the single-page note and handed it to her husband. He carefully held it up and read its deftly scrawled message. It was addressed to:

Reporter for the King—Samuel Antonius

You ask yourself, "Was it real? Was it really all a dream?" Your life in the present day—does it not also seem like a dream? You will necessarily be the judge of this.

You were charged with a promise to make a report and accepted this charge with the faith of a child. For what you have done this day you will forever be known by title: *Samuel— Reporter for the King!*

You have made *The Christ Report* a worldwide event and now Cleopas is finally at peace. And our King? He wishes a sacred message for you, one He hopes you learned walking with us from Jerusalem to Emmaus. The message is one of hope. Hope springs from a knowledge that God is always there with His loving concern for each mortal as a parent does love each of his children individually.

Our King is of Heaven, but He planted this earth in its place for one purpose; that purpose is "experience" for His children that they may grow in peace and love, and that they may experience it most fully. To do so they must choose the source of all love.

Our King, unlike those of His day when he walked with us on the road to Emmaus, is filled with grace, mercy, love, and ever invites us with an outstretched hand of nail prints, in hopes that we might believe. For this to come to pass, one must simply seek Him, and then He will appear.

Where shall this appearance be? Here is the secret, and the mystery to all faith. As it was on the road to Emmaus, so may it be for every man and woman.

Samuel, who healed your broken heart? Who mended your skeptical mind? Who caused the blind man within to see? Who promised you the love you feel as you hold your wife's hand and also now, as you read these words?

What happened to Cleopas and I on the way to Emmaus can happen for anyone who seeks Him with a sincere and broken heart. Do you not recall the words our friend Luke wrote? Those words Cleopas and I used to confirm his personal appearance?

"Did not our hearts burn within us, while he talked with us by the way?"

Now you too know how to find Him anytime, on any road of life you may travel upon. Now you know He will hear you! The world has waited long to know this, as if it were a secret. It need not be secret anymore! Continue to report this yielding of the broken and contrite heart to the Master, and then the world may itself feel His fire that restores and renews!

Cleopas thanks you for keeping your pledge to him and he now keeps his to you. I have been entrusted with a token of respect from our mutual friend, the Innkeeper of Emmaus. You will have found carefully wrapped in woolen cloth something special and kept from the world until this day. Once crafted by a carpenter's son, this carved fir wood tablet from Mt. Tabor was a reminder, hung atop the entrance of a humble inn destroyed by fire in the town of our Master's birth. This alone, survived the blaze of the first inn of Bethlehem, and was kept safe near Emmaus until this day.

Let this token assure you that your visit was no night vision alone, but a journey to a time and place that really did happen. You, Samuel, kept not only a promise to Cleopas but to your new Lord and God.

Shalom, Brother Samuel Antonius. May peace and love grace your house forevermore!

In the service of our King! Friend Cornelius

"It was a dream!" he gasped.

"Samuel?" Rachel pressed. She stood to steady him. "You're trembling. Should I call a doctor?"

"No," he blurted, barely able to speak. He gazed up at the ceiling, as if seeking an answer hidden there. He brushed at his eyes, thinking to stop the damn bursting from them. A low moan emanated from his chest, a sob deep from within.

Rachel, frightened, now stroked his arm. "Here... Honey, please... Sit. Tell me what it is."

He held up his hand to assure her that he was okay. Then he cradled the sacred object in both hands and reread the words from his dreamland friend.

At last, he wiped his eyes with his sleeve and he made his way past the sliding door glass out onto the balcony. The snow was falling heavier now—large, satin flakes gliding down from a translucent sky. He leaned on the railing and scanned the quiet, abandoned streets below for any sign of *him*. His gaze led him to a tall man in the plaza that fronted the mall on the opposite corner. Shrouded in a billowing overcoat, a hood obscured his features, excepting a pair of steady eyes fixed on Sam.

"*You!*"

The tall man slowly brought his hand up in greeting, his elbow at a right angle, in a salute of friendship. As he did so, Sam fully expected the apparition to disappear, as he had just an hour earlier. But the man, after returning Sam's salutation, reached up and removed the hood from his head – to reveal himself a sure witness indeed to what had transpired. Then he smiled, nodded, and turned, before dissolving into the snowy whiteness that enveloped New York this Christmas Eve.

"Sam? Who was that?" Rachel sidled up from behind, her arms wrapping around him, hands clasped over his chest.

He could barely get the words out. "*A Friend,*" he exclaimed in reverence.

He and Rachel remained in each other's embrace for several long, wordless minutes. His eyes continued to sweep the street below, straining to see past the increasingly dense screen of falling flakes. At last, she suggested they return to the warmth of the cozy, dry apartment. He finally relented and followed her inside.

Sam earlier had supposed that he was happy, and supremely so. But now he was more - he was, in a word, *fulfilled*. An indescribable peace swept over him as he understood that some things simply don't have easy answers; that reality is what we *believe and feel* more than what we simply *see*.

Taking tools from the kitchen drawer, he fastened the ancient wood plaque above their entry door. Then he stepped back for Rachel to see. "It should hang here forever," he said, finally finding his voice. "When we enter, when we depart, it will remind us..."

"Sam, what does it say? The language is not familiar. And why has it touched you so deeply?"

"There *was* an inn in ancient Bethlehem, Rachel. A carpenter's son carved these words into a board that his cousin, the innkeeper, had hung above his door. He kept it there to remind him of their kinship."

He paused and looked Rachel in the eye, a profound sense of reverence in his gaze. "The inscription is taken from the Koheleth, the words of Ecclesiastes, also called the 'Preacher'..." His voice caught and he bowed his head, unable to finish.

"Sam," whispered Rachel, reaching up to brush the tears away. She pulled his face down to hers, stroking his quivering cheeks, kissing away the wetness on them. "How can I help?"

For another long moment, husband and wife held one another. Then Sam made the attempt to answer Rachel's question. "Never doubt. Always believe," he said, simply. "Love me and remind me of this day forever," he ended.

She simply nodded as if he should continue.

Then he looked up at the plaque once again. "The innkeeper said he would give this to me if I did my report, if I revealed to the world the truth about his devotion to his Master."

He closed his watery eyes, squeezing one more salty droplet from each. He knew the words from his dream *by heart*. They had brought him back to his beloved. "If it had not been for them, for that place, for Him... I couldn't be..." he stopped and drank a deep breath of emotion filled air into his lungs, "...I couldn't be here with you today," he said turning to her.

Rachel didn't understand all of what he said but whispered, "I feel what you are saying. Right here," she softly said, gently patting her chest.

Sam nodded. *That's right my love. That's right*, he thought to himself as he tenderly kissed her cheek and set his head against hers. He gazed, eyes wide open and far beyond this moment, as he embraced Rachel. His new faith had made him whole, complete, and gave him a new set of eyes; those discerning from his heart where all truth can appear with unfettered rationalization—a place where the mind of Christ is born, lives, and speaks.

As if seeing the words on the plaque for the first time, there in the presence of Cleopas at the dim but warmly lit Inn of Emmaus, he now uttered them aloud, each word, slowly, respectfully:

"Go thy way, eat and drink with joy, and drink thy wine with a merry heart, for God now accepteth thy works. Live joyfully with the wife whom thou lovest...
for that is thy portion in this life..."

AUTHOR'S AFTERWORD

THE CHRIST REPORT is a work of fiction. However, the characters Cleopas, Cornelius, and others are taken from the dramatic accounts as found in the Holy Bible. I have exclusively used the most widely read and time-honored version of the Holy Bible for reference; the nearly five hundred year-old King James Version.

I have taken great pains to not use religious bias but be a storyteller; simply true to the purity found in this classical version of the Bible text yet wondering what "might have been" as between the lines I read what was reported by Luke in his Gospel.

Liberties for purposes of storytelling are of my own making in an effort to add to the world's great body of entertaining work regarding the inspiring accounts of one Holy Birth, Crucifixion, and Resurrection of Him who I honor as the Christ, the Light of the World, and Lord; even Jesus of Nazareth.

For more background on the writing of this novel, and for a free download of the bestselling *Ultimate Bible Study Suite, I* invite you to my website www.powerthink.com.

-James Michael Pratt 2008

ABOUT THE AUTHOR

New York Times and *USA Today* bestselling author, James Michael Pratt is the author of nine published works, including soon-to-be CBS Hallmark Hall of Fame based upon his first international release, *The Last Valentine.* His family-friendly novels delving into the complexities of war, love and relationships, and history have earned him the accolades of critics. *Booklist* called him, "A master of moral fiction." *Publisher's Weekly* said of *The Lighthouse Keeper*, "His simple story will please the readers ready for a good cry." His novels have reached a worldwide audience. Pratt's other bestsellers in hardcover and paperback also include:

- *Ticket Home*
- *Paradise Bay*
- DAD, *The Man Who Lied to Save the Planet*
- MOM, *The Woman Who Made Oatmeal Stick to My Ribs*

The Christ Report, along with his latest work of inspirational fiction released in Spring 2008, *As a Man Thinketh...In His Heart*, take readers by the hand into a world of possibilities where faith blends with answers to some of life's most perplexing questions about meaning and what matters most.

James and his wife Jeanne have been married thirty years. He is a partner in a company, PowerThink, LLC, devoted to inspiration and self-improvement. For more about his life and writings please visit: www.powerthink.com and his personal website, www.jmpratt.com.

BESTSELLERS FROM
POWERTHINK™ PUBLISHING

HEARTLAND BOOKS

from
PowerThink™ Publishing

BESTSELLING INSPIRATIONAL FICTION

By

James Michael Pratt

New York Times and *USA TODAY*
Bestselling Author

AS a MAN THINKETH...In His Heart

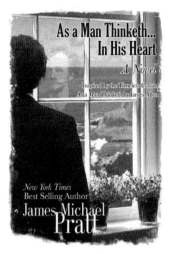

New York Times and *USA TODAY* bestselling author, James Michael Pratt, known for his heart-warming stories of love, faith, and historic laden plots offers an unforgettable journey to a time and place that has stood still. Hyrum Smith, Co-Founder of Franklin Covey said: *"As a Man Thinketh In His Heart* **is a fascinating continuation of the ideas set forth in James Allen's** *As a Man Thinketh.* **Mr. Pratt takes those principles of thought and adds to it the principles of heart powered thinking. He does it in such an engaging way that the reader is greatly entertained while pondering the power of thought and its relationship with the heart. Whoever reads this will be infused with not only the desire to change for the better, but the belief that positive change is possible."**

Millions of readers have credited the reading of James Allen's non-fiction treatise, *As a Man Thinketh* (1902), as a changing point in their lives. Millions of copies are in print worldwide. Now, 100 years later, another James brings the gentle spirit of philosopher/author Allen alive in, *As a Man Thinketh...In His Heart.*

Novelist James Michael Pratt was deeply touched by Allen's book when he received it on his nineteenth birthday; a gift from his mother and father. Allen's inspiring words, among others, moved Pratt to chart a course which ultimately led to his becoming an author of inspirational fiction and non-fiction.

The lovers of James Allen's work will be thrilled as James Pratt goes on the hunt for the mysterious writer of a partially completed turn-of-the-century manuscript, *Hampton of Devon*, which he hopes is available for his use as a new novel. His search for the copyright leads him to Ilfracombe, England, hometown and last residence of author James Allen. Little will Pratt realize that time has been suspended at an obscure cottage, over-looking the Atlantic, and that answers to some of life's most important questions will be given him by the owner, a humble man of modest means. Pratt will come away from the experience with far more than he bargained for in a simple research trip.

The pleasant stay, at what Pratt knew as a remote hillside Bed and Breakfast in Ilfracombe, is nothing short of a miraculous transfer of information desperately needed for a world living at break-neck speed, self-destructive in its cerebral approach to life's urgent problems, and dying from a lack of direction the proprietor of the Victorian era cottage alone may offer.

As a Man Thinketh...In His Heart holds secrets for the reader to a better way to live as it reunites millions with the beloved, but obscure Englishman Allen, who bequeathed a treasure trove of inspiration before dying in 1912. But perhaps death is not what it seems, and great thinkers of yesterday have barely begun their work...

THE CHRIST REPORT

A story of the Holy Birth, Passion, Hidden Secrets, and Everlasting Hope

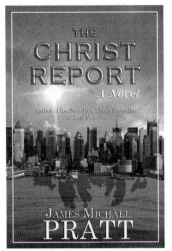

Destined to become a Christmas classic and Easter perennial, *The Christ Report* is a magical tale told from the perspective of radio and television host Sam Robertson of CNTV's Robertson Reports, readers go on a journey of imagination; interviews and being interviewed in the year 30 AD. Or was it simple imagination? After all the name and places come from the Gospel of Luke and it all seems so real...

Readers and reviewers of James Michael Pratt's first inspirational/religious fiction have said:

- "I loved it! Can't wait to share with my family and friends."
- "Old and young are going to enjoy this Christmas and Easter tale. A must read!"
- "I couldn't put it down. It really touched me."
- "The story of Christ's birth and death has never been told from this perspective before. I was thoroughly captivated."

Story Summary:

A secret kept since the Holy Birth will be revealed when two men, separated by two thousand years in time, search for a meaning greater than themselves. Both suffer from broken hearts, yearn to keep the women they love, and worry about their legacy. One, Sam Robertson, the world-famous host of CNTV's *The Sam Robertson Report*, will soon find that only a life-saving miracle can bring him the hope his sense of self-importance cannot offer.

The other man, battered by regrets as ancient as the biblical story in which he played a key role, once was an innkeeper – indeed, the very one who had rejected the parents of an infant destined to become immortalized as the Son of God in countless pageants and dramas. Now it's the innkeeper's charge to convey a vital message to the world, a message that has been kept hidden for two millennia.

This secret, kept even from those who understand the stories of the Holy Birth and the Passion, was not so much a secret that must not be known, but, rather, something *sacred*, kept hidden for so long because of mankind's self-serving stubbornness.

Now, not only will Sam land the interview of a lifetime, but he'll win another chance at life and love. And Cleopas the Innkeeper will likewise gain a second opportunity to redeem his soul and clear his name as the most vilified innkeeper of all time.

Their secret? It is only to be found in *The Christ Report*.

THE GOOD HEART

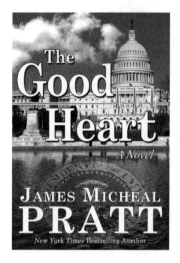

A James Pratt novel, *The Good Heart* (hardcover) was heralded as a:

"Political thriller with a moral twist," and "…fast paced, I couldn't it down."—KSL AM 1160 radio host and film critic Doug Wright.

A story of love, broken hearts, transplants, cellular memories of murder, deceit, and honor takes you on a roller coaster ride for 298 pages. A film script has been optioned by Ridini Entertainment of LA and New York.

THE STORY:

When a hard-living political hack and Washington DC insider, Mike Stone, finally finds the love of his life, Dr. Maggie Sanders, his physical heart is failing. Powerful US Senator Joseph Caine and his cronies bidding for the White House need the knowledge stored in Mike's head.

But to keep it alive they will need to make sure he gets a "good heart." A Floridian pastor and the senator's brother, Nicholas Caine, is dying. He graciously agrees to donate any organ that may aid another soul. Within Nick's heart are memories of dark years he and his Southern Senator brother had lived as younger men.

Mike Stone will receive a medical first…Pastor Nick Caine's second-hand heart. With the new heart also comes startling memories and revelations hidden from the public's knowledge. Memories stored in a heart transferred from one James Barlow, black Southern minister from the civil rights era to Nick Caine, his former antagonist, and now to Mike Stone, cold and calculating political aide to the senator.

When the transplant gives Mike Stone a second chance at life, the heart memories from two men; those of murder, intrigue, regrets, now may cost Mike his healthy life, and the only thing that now matters more than that – his love for Maggie Sanders, their new family, and the truth.

Coming Summer of 2008

HEARTLAND BOOKS

from
PowerThink™ Publishing

BESTSELLING INSPIRATIONAL NON FICTION

By

James Michael Pratt

New York Times and *USA TODAY*
Bestselling Author

DAD, The Man Who Lied to Save the Planet

12 Timeless Virtues Handed Down to a Son by an Everyday Dad

"For anyone who admits to having forgotten the important things of life, James Michael Pratt,s *DAD, The Man Who Lied to Save the Planet* is here to remind you."
—Kenneth J. Atchity, President, AEI Film producer and bestselling author.

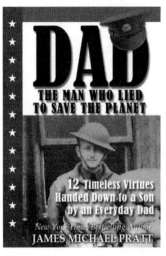

In this loving tribute to his dad, *New York Times* and *USA TODAY* bestselling author, James Michael Pratt evokes a simpler time in American history—the years following the Great Depression and World War Two, when Southern California was still filled with dusty little towns and when a man could have purchased bean fields that have become LA International Airport fir $5 dollars an acre, except few had five dollars to spare.

A veteran of World War Two and a member of the generation Tom Brokaw called "the greatest generation," skinny Grant Pratt lied about his weight to enlist in the Army at the outbreak of war in 1941. An unpretentious man who acquired little of the world's wealth, what he did possess in rich abundance was a wit and wisdom built upon old-fashioned values, and which he somehow succeeded in passing along to his family of ten children—values readers today will no doubt find refreshing.

In conclusion to the stirring tribute to the 12 time-tested values as demonstrated in life, Pratt recounts the final minutes of his father's life. As Grant struggled to breathe, and gasped for air to utter final words his lungs and tongue had not possessed strength to do, the author offers a glimpse at what really matters most:

"My father groaned, struggling to form something with his lips, but unable to do so. He could barely raise an eyelid now but kept trying to speak, at least with his eyes. Mom said a tearful good-bye as she stroked his head and kissed him over and over. I sat at his left, holding his hand. 'You can go now Grant. You can go, darling,' she said.

"Even if he had been able to speak top his wife, her deafness would have prevented her from receiving the offering. He closed his moist eyes and tears drained from their corners as his pulse steadily weakened. *So this is how Dad dies. Congratulations, Dad. You won the fight,* I thought. I didn't expect more from him. But suddenly…"

James Michael Pratt pulls at the heart-strings until the end as he relates the miracle expression of three sacred words given to a father for a final gift to a son. Through the heart-warming stories and nostalgic reflections, James Pratt reminds us that twelve timeless virtues are in an increasing short supply in today's world. In doing so, he reaffirms for today's dads the unique power a father has to shape and mold his children's characters and touch lives even after his own life ends.

MOM, The Woman Who Made Oatmeal Stick to My Ribs

12 Lessons of Life a Son Learned to Love

"If you enjoyed Tuesdays with Morrie, you're going to love this book! It's packed with inspiring words of wisdom, not just for mothers but for everyone."
—Gary and Joy Lundberg, bestselling authors of
I Don't Have to Make Everything All Better

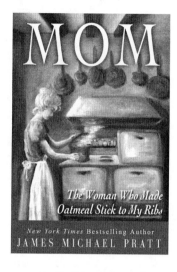

"Oatmeal might not really stick to ribs, but I never, ever eat it without hearing Mom's voice. So it wasn't just the oatmeal that stuck to this boy. The porridge was a symbol of something else that would stay with me—her love and pride in me and the time-tested values she taught, which provided real warmth and a shield against the punches life would deliver." Such is the influence of mothers as told by *New York Times* bestselling author James Michael Pratt in his warm-hearted tribute to his own mother. His nostalgic reflections on his own upbringing will recall Mom's admonitions to, "Eat your food. There are starving Children in Africa," and "Do unto others as you want to do to you. Hardcover publisher Shadow Mountain called Pratt's memoir, "Funny, poignant, and uplifting…and a perfect tribute to any mother."

As Pratt leads the reader to a heart-touching conclusion through his own mind's eye, we understand that we can go home anytime we want by simply recalling the warmth of the home cooking, the caring of a mother eager and concerned over her brood:

"Mom, we say good-bye to you when we grow up, but you never leave us alone. Your face, your voice, your love, echoes throughout our lives, calling us back to simpler days and times. Now and then we come home in our mind's eyes. You are there waiting with good food and a warm heart. We are listening to you, feeling your tender embrace, the kiss on our cheek, and our hearts are gladdened. Mom, I'm closing my eyes now…"

MOM, The Woman Who Made Oatmeal Stick to My Ribs is now available in audio book and paperback. This and other inspirational Pratt titles are published by Heartland Books, a division of PowerThink Publishing, LLC.

POWERTHINK™ PUBLISHING

BESTSELLING NON FICTION
SELF-IMPROVEMENT

The DRUG of the New Millennium
The Brain Science Behind Internet Pornography Use

The most devastating "super-drug" in history is attacking our children and teenagers!
3 Power Principles will protect those you love.

Included in the back of the book:
Special 70-minute Audio Training CD from Mark Kastleman:
"PROTECTING FAMILIES FROM THE HARMFUL EFFECTS OF MEDIA & TECHNOLOGY"

Mark B. Kastleman
Foreword by Dr. Randall F. Hyde

An epidemic is sweeping across America and much of the world. Parents and spouses are desperate for answers. Clergy and counselors are inundated and searching for solutions. It's estimated that over 60 million in the U.S. are addicted at some level. Nine out of ten children between age eight and sixteen have been exposed. Teens are the largest consumers. The epidemic?—**Internet Pornography Use.** Now, via computers, cell phones and even video gaming systems, every variety of Internet porn is instantly available to anyone, regardless of age or gender—no one is immune!

After 10 years of study and research with leading neuro-scientists, and direct interaction with more than 10,000 families, renowned author, researcher and speaker Mark B. Kastleman brings the world his groundbreaking work. Rather than approaching this controversial issue from the traditional moral or religious angle, Mark sticks to the facts—the "brain science" behind Internet pornography use. For example:

Internet porn triggers a flood-release of potent neuro-chemicals in the brain virtually identical to illicit street drugs. Porn use is "substance-abuse"—a "drug addiction."

Internet pornography radically alters the brain at cellular level, dramatically impacting attitudes and behaviors.

Most importantly, in addition to cutting-edge brain science, Mark provides parents, spouses, clergy and counselors with the **3 Power Principles guaranteed** to protect children, marriages and families—**tested and proven practical solutions** to prevent addiction to this "super-drug."

This remarkable, comprehensive guidebook gives people the straight-forward, no-nonsense answers and practical solutions they've been searching for.

Reviews:

"Through computer and cell phone Internet use, kids and adults are exposed to extreme media that radically alters the brain and dramatically impacts behavior!" "Families must use the *3 Power Principles* in this book to protect themselves from these devastating influences."
—DR. RANDALL F. HYDE, NATIONALLY RENOWNED CHILD PSYCHOLOGIST

"Kastleman has presented a masterful analysis of how pornography destroys the mental and spiritual capacity of its victim. I recommend this outstanding book to all parents, educators and religious leaders."
—JOHN L. HARMER, FORMER LT. GOVERNOR OF CALIFORNIA UNDER RONALD REAGAN

"Mark's book is a wonderful resource and guide for those desiring to protect their families from this terrible plague."
—DR. VICTOR CLINE, PROFESSOR EMERITIS OF PSYCHOLOGY, UNIVERSITY OF UTAH

"This is one of the most important books of this decade. Many families and marriages will be saved through the careful reading and application of this remarkable book."
—DR. PAGE BAILEY, WORLD-RENOWNED NEUROPSYCHOLOGIST

"Kastleman's work on mind/body responses to pornography is cutting-edge.
—DR. JUDITH REISMAN, AUTHOR OF *SOFT PORNO PLAYS*

POWERTHINK™ PUBLISHING

BESTSELLING NON FICTION
FINANCE & LIVING

Nominated for the 2008 Pulitzer Prize
ENDING GLOBAL POVERTY
The MicroFranchise Solution

ENDING GLOBAL POVERTY – The MicroFranchise Solution by Kirk Magleby has been nominated for a Pulitzer Prize. This groundbreaking book helps the reader discover the fundamental root causes of poverty while illuminating the solution. Mr. Magleby has captured the imaginations of audiences worldwide with his solutions, and now offers in an articulate and intelligent fashion, the easy-to-read formula for ending the scourge of global poverty. Readers have said:

"I am hugely impressed. This is exactly the kind of foreign aid in which I myself deeply believe." —Jay Ambrose, Chief Editorial Writer, Scripps Howard News Service

"This is precisely what we need in this country." —Maximo San Roman, Peru, former Vice President of Peru, Founder, Nova Industries

"Language which is sure to illuminate for many what is possible in terms of doing business with and improving life for some of the poorest people on the planet." —Barbara Weber, Grameen Foundation, USA

Over 500,000 copies of the content found in this first edition, 200-page treatment have been downloaded off various internet sites since October, 2005 including the concise quick-read article entitled, *MicroFranchises as a Solution to World Poverty*, first submitted to the *2006 World Bank/Financial Times* essay competition on private sector solutions to poverty. The online download has helped launch dozens of MicroFranchise projects worldwide using the scalable business model pioneered by the various Grameen Enterprises of which Muhammad Yunus, 2006 Nobel Peace Prize winner, said: *"That is what we are doing It works. Just go do it."*

Kirk Magleby with
Nobel Peace Prize winner,
Dr. Muhammad Yunus

Others have said:

"I really enjoyed this book. I sent it to several colleagues within my company as well as external partners who are engaged in various MicroFranchises in India."
—Karishma Kiri, Emerging Markets, Microsoft

"Very impressive. I have been overwhelmed, in a positive way. Thank you for your most significant contribution to a bare cupboard of literature on such a potentially world-changing subject."
—Stephen W. Gibson, Entrepreneur in Residence, Marriott School of Management, BYU

"First rate piece of work. The footnotes are almost better than the book itself."
—Dwight Wilson, CEO, OneRoof

"Articulate, stimulating. One of the best books in years. The footnotes are the finest short course on development available today."
—John Hatch, Washington, D.C., founder, FINCA, Microfinance pioneer

<u>FREE AUDIO CD:</u> Each trade paperback copy comes with a FREE audio CD of the exclusive 45-minute interview with author/world-renowned humanitarian, Kirk Magleby. Kirk clearly explores the causes and cures of global poverty including information on what any individual can do to participate.

World's Definitive e-Book Collection

Over 60,000 e-Books for the computer and mobile device!

One Collection Includes 6 Large Libraries for the Computer and Handheld Device

The Complete Christian Collection - 2005 Edition

Includes 350 works of the most popular Bibles, commentaries, reference, and inspirational works ever published. With this library you will be able to easily peruse the works of the greatest Bible scholars who ever lived.

- 350 Volumes in 14 Collections
- Over 5 Million Cross-Reference Links

- Powerful Search Tool: Search by Author, Title, Collection and more
- Quickly and easily lookup a scripture, topic, Bible Dictionary entry and more
- Fully-linked Nave's Topical Bible with over 34,000 topics
- Fully-linked Torrey's Topical Textbook with over 21,000 topics
- Fully-linked Hebrew/Greek Dictionary & Concordance
- Customize your library with personal notes, highlighters, and bookmarks
- Export, Save, and Print
- Over 60 Full-Color Maps
- Gazetteer Linked to over 1,200 Bible Locations
- #1 Rated Folio® search software.
- All this and much more

American Freedom Library

Over 60,000 key works, documents, and histories. Never before have so many works been so easily accessible. Includes the Presidential Papers from Washington to Bush, 1,000 Landmark Supreme Court cases,1,100 original source accounts throughout history, over 15,000 famous quotes, and much more. Feel the pulse of history through some of the greatest works of American history.

- Over 60,000 Works in 9 collections
- Each title is indexed for easy search & navigation
- Smart Search by Collection, Title, and more.
- Smart Lookup key events in history, speeches, Supreme Court cases, famous quotes and more
- Includes 95 Lesson Plans featuring source-document learning activities
- Customize your library with personal notes, highlighters, and bookmarks
- Export, Save, and Print for use in school, speeches, and more
- #1 Rated Folio® search software.
- All this and much more

Ultimate Classic Library

Includes over 1,000 works of the most popular writers. Never before have so many works been so easily accessible. With this library you will be able to easily peruse the works of the greatest writers who ever lived. From Charles Dickens to William Shakespeare... from Louis May Alcott to Lucy Maud Montgomery, this is the largest library of it's kind and a must for your software collection.

- Over 1,000 works
- Each title is indexed for easy navigation
- Search by Author, Title, Collection, or any combination.
- Easy search (word combinations, phrases, and more)
- Customize your library with personal notes, highlighters, and bookmarks
- Export, Save, and Print for use in school, speeches, studies and more
- Includes Drama, Poetry, Biography, Philosophy, Inspiration, Adventure, and much more
- #1 Rated Folio® search software.
- All this and much more!

One Million Recipes

Over 1,070,000 Recipes

Search for title, ingredient, content, and preparation methods by word.

Nutritional Information: Over 6,000 of the most commonly used ingredients, with complete nutritional data on the following:

- Calories
- Vitamins
- Proteins

- Carbohydrates
- Fats/Cholesterol
- Sodium and Fiber
- 52 Recipe Categories
- Each category is indexed for easy navigation
- Add, customize, and edit new recipes
- Save recipes either as a file for editing or print them out on a standard 8.5"x11" notebook format.
- Calendar/Meal Planner
- Print your recipes or copy and paste them to your word processor
- All this and much more!

Quote Master

Includes over 50,000 of the world's most popular quotes. Never before have so many quotes been so easily accessible. Great for talks, business presentations, lectures, school reports, essays, motivational speeches, building vocabulary, counseling, encouragement, humor, spiritual enrichment, sales presentations and everyday conversations.

- Over 50,000 quotes
- Indexed for easy navigation
- Easy search by word, phrase, topic, author, bio, and source
- Print the quotes you want
- Copy and save the quotes you want to your word processor document.
- Topics include love, marriage, God, money, happiness, patience, hope, wisdom, business, death, reason, virtue, and many more
- Add your own or other quotes you want to the library
- All this and much more!

Complete Herbal Reference Library

Indexes over 2,500 herbs, vitamins and minerals. Over 2,500 recipes, tinctures, and formulas. Over 250 full color and black/white photos. Over 12,000 cross-reference links with expert commentary. Over 2,500 herbs, vitamins, and minerals.

- Over 2,500 recipes
- Expert Commentary
- Indexed for easy navigation
- Search by Author, Title, Collection, or any combination.
- Easy search (word combinations, phrases, and more)
- Customize your library with personal notes, highlighters, and bookmarks
- Export, Save, and Print for use in school, speeches, studies and more
- #1 Rated Folio® search software.
- All this and much more!
-

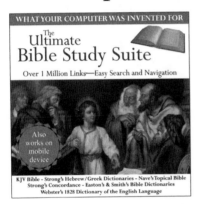